Endorsements

"Who better to write a book on the gospel than John Mac-Arthur? This master expositor and skilled theologian has spent his entire ministry defining and defending the one, true, saving gospel of Jesus Christ. In these pages, you will discover the biblical basis for the good news of salvation that is in the person and work of the Son of God, Jesus Christ. Your heart will be thrilled as you behold the glory of God in the image of Him who is the only Savior of sinners, the Lord of heaven and earth. Here is yet another doctrinally profound yet easily accessible book by this best-selling author. Whatever MacArthur writes, read it for the good of your soul. This book is no exception."

—DR. STEVEN J. LAWSON
President, OnePassion Ministries
Dallas

"In this important book, John MacArthur unpacks the gospel by drawing attention to its heart and essence—Jesus. Nothing is more important for us to know and understand than the gospel. Without this understanding, we are in danger of being eternally lost. You may think you are thoroughly familiar with the gospel, but this book can show you aspects of it that you may have missed. And crucially, these chapters are all about Jesus—who He is, who He claimed to be, what He came to do, and what He accomplished. Whether you are reading MacArthur for the first time or the hundredth, you will not be disappointed."

—DR. DEREK W.H. THOMAS
Senior Minister, First Presbyterian Church
Columbia, S.C.

GOOD NEWS

GOOD NEWS

THE GOSPEL OF JESUS CHRIST

JOHN MACARTHUR

Reformation Trust   A DIVISION OF LIGONIER MINISTRIES, ORLANDO, FL

Good News: The Gospel of Jesus Christ
© 2018 by John MacArthur

Published by Reformation Trust Publishing
A division of Ligonier Ministries
421 Ligonier Court, Sanford, FL 32771
Ligonier.org   ReformationTrust.com

Printed in York, Pennsylvania
Maple Press
March 2018
First edition, second printing

978-1-56769-856-5 (Hardcover)
978-1-56769-924-1 (ePub)
978-1-56769-925-8 (Kindle)

Cover design by Metaleap Creative.
Interior design and typeset: Katherine Lloyd, The DESK

Unless otherwise indicated, Scripture quotations are from the New American Standard Bible® (NASB), Copyright © 1960, 1962, 1963, 1968, 1971, 1972, 1973, 1975, 1977, 1995 by The Lockman Foundation. Used by permission. www.Lockman.org

Scripture quotations marked (KJV) are from the King James Version. Public domain.

Library of Congress Cataloging-in-Publication Data
Names: MacArthur, John, 1939- author.
Title: Good news : the Gospel of Jesus Christ / John MacArthur.
Description: Orlando, FL : Reformation Trust Publishing, 2018. | Includes bibliographical references and index.
Identifiers: LCCN 2017032623 | ISBN 9781567698565
Subjects: LCSH: Jesus Christ--Person and offices.
Classification: LCC BT203 .M245 2018 | DDC 232--dc23
LC record available at https://lccn.loc.gov/2017032623:

CONTENTS

Chapter One

JESUS
IS THE MESSIAH

Who is Jesus? It's a very basic question, but one that many struggle to answer. Virtually all the world's religions and philosophies attempt to identify Him: as a gentle prophet, a faithful wise man, a spiritual teacher, or a social revolutionary ahead of His time. Others position Him as a sorcerer or a demigod, with access to supernatural power but subordinate to a greater divine overseer. Still others skirt the biblical accounts, treating Jesus as a great man whose legend has grown through myth and folklore—almost like a first-century Paul Bunyan.

Even the cults attempt to identify who or what Christ was. Take Scientology, for example, the pseudo-religion popularized in recent years by several Hollywood celebrities. Scientology is a demonically informed system invented by a science-fiction writer and medium named L. Ron Hubbard. According to Hubbard, Jesus never existed as a person. Instead, Christ is an electronic idea implanted by the true powers of the universe as a type of cosmic disinformation campaign. In a letter to his followers, dated May 5, 1980, Hubbard wrote, "Let me take the opportunity to disabuse you of some lovely myths. For instance, the historic Jesus was not nearly the sainted figure he has been made out to be. In addition to being a lover of young boys and men, he was given to uncontrollable bursts of temper and hatred that belied the general message of love."[1]

It's difficult to imagine anything more bizarre or blasphemous than that. Yet if people reject the true Christ of Scripture, any replacement they concoct with their imaginations—while potentially less outrageous than Hubbard's version—won't be any less erroneous or heretical. Even if they have differing notions, everyone who rejects the biblical truth about Christ inevitably ends up in a similar place. The effect of missing the truth about the Lord is always the same, since anything other than believing in the true Christ is a damning offense.

Moreover, the right understanding of Jesus Christ is essential to understanding many other vital truths, particularly the gospel and salvation. There's no good news apart from Christ. Jesus Himself warned His followers not to fall for "false Christs" (Mark 13:21–22). In 2 John 10–11, the Apostle of love says that anyone who departs from the true doctrine of Christ does not have God; therefore, "if anyone comes to you and does not bring this teaching, do not receive him into your house, and do not give him a greeting; for the one who gives him a greeting participates in his evil deeds." Clearly, how you answer the question "Who is Jesus?" has significant and ultimately permanent consequences. The right answer *alone* can lead to salvation. Yet one can be very close to the right answer and still miss it, resulting in eternal disaster.

What Did Jesus Say about Himself?

One way to answer the question "Who is Jesus?" is by listening to His monumental words to the scribes in the temple, recorded in Luke's gospel:

> Then He said to them, "How is it that they say the Christ is David's son? For David himself says in the book of Psalms,
>
> 'The Lord said to my Lord,
> "Sit at My right hand,
> Until I make Your enemies a footstool for Your feet."'
>
> Therefore David calls Him 'Lord,' and how is He his son?"
>
> And while all the people were listening, He said to the disciples, "Beware of the scribes, who like to walk around in long robes, and love respectful greetings in the market places, and chief seats in the synagogues and places of honor at banquets, who devour widows' houses, and for appearance's sake offer long prayers. These will receive greater condemnation."
>
> And He looked up and saw the rich putting their gifts into the treasury. And He saw a poor widow

putting in two small copper coins. And He said, "Truly I say to you, this poor widow put in more than all of them; for they all out of their surplus put into the offering; but she out of her poverty put in all that she had to live on."

And while some were talking about the temple, that it was adorned with beautiful stones and votive gifts, He said, "As for these things which you are looking at, the days will come in which there will not be left one stone upon another which will not be torn down." (Luke 20:41–21:6)

Many people today think that if they get most things right—even if they miss on "the Jesus part"—they're still going to heaven. That's the new breadth of tolerance that defines much of contemporary evangelicalism, which effectively opens a back door to heaven. It's the revival of an ancient lie: you don't have to believe specifically in Christ. As long as you're a monotheist and believe in the one true God (and *especially* if you believe in the God of Abraham, Isaac, and Jacob), you're going to be fine.

This mind-set is diametrically opposed to what we read in Luke's gospel. Jesus warns the Jews who have made the wrong conclusions about Him that they will not enjoy a lesser condemnation. In fact, not only will they *not* receive salvation, not only will they *not* be excused, but they will receive a *greater* condemnation. That ought to be a sobering message for people today who are trying to extend and expand the gospel to include anyone who believes in God—any god—as long as it's a monotheistic system. And it ought to terrify everyone who presumes that God's standards are as fluid and flexible as twenty-first-century tolerance is.

At the time of Christ's statements in Luke 20–21, Judaism was on the brink of an imminent disaster—one in which the symbol of this religious system, the temple, was going to be leveled. Standing in the shadow of the temple, the Lord Jesus Himself was warning anyone who would listen that divine condemnation was coming on the apostate form of Judaism. Remember, this was not some pagan or pantheistic religion He was condemning. They believed in the one true and living God: the God who was the Creator; the God who spoke in the Old Testament; the God who revealed Himself through the prophets and His righteous character through the law; and the God who established that He would uphold His righteous character by means of judgment. The Jews readily affirmed all the truths about God found in the Old Testament.

But it was not enough. Jesus never sat down and said, "You know, we've got so much common ground; let's find a connection and have a conversation about the truths we can mutually affirm." He wasn't interested in identifying common ground or accommodating ignorance. Only the truth—the full truth—could set an Israelite or anyone else free from the slavery of sin.

Setting the Scene

As we consider this brief episode from Luke's gospel, let's establish what has already occurred. The Lord is at the end of His three-year earthly ministry. He has traversed Judea and Galilee and has gone from town to village to city proclaiming the gospel of the kingdom, banishing illness, demonstrating divine power over demons, and repeatedly declaring Himself as the fulfillment of Old Testament messianic prophecy. He has been proclaiming that He is not only the Messiah but also God, and He has proved it through His power over nature, disease, demons, and even death. But now, after three years, His public ministry is finished.

When we pick up the story in Luke 20, it is Wednesday of Passion Week. On the previous Saturday, "six days before the Passover" (John 12:1), He had first come through Jericho, ascended to Jerusalem, and arrived at Bethany. That evening, He found His place of rest with His friends Mary, Martha, and Lazarus—whose emergence from the grave had stirred up no small amount of conversation in Jerusalem. In fact, it was largely the resurrection of Lazarus that drew the crowds (v. 9). The crowds were still teeming a day or two later when He entered Jerusalem triumphantly. He rode "on a colt, the foal of a donkey," because that is what Zechariah 9:9 said He would do. He came into Jerusalem fulfilling prophecy.

The crowds were massive; some would estimate a quarter-million people were there. It was a real possibility in their minds that He might be the long-awaited Messiah. What else could explain His power and His authoritative proclamation of the truth? He spoke like no man had ever spoken (John 7:46). And the crowd was at a fever pitch because He had raised Lazarus from the dead.

Jesus came back into town early on Tuesday after having departed Monday night to go to the Mount of Olives. Each night He stayed on the Mount of Olives—He took His disciples through the eastern gate of Jerusalem, walked down the little slope, crossed the Kidron brook, went up the Mount of Olives directly east of Jerusalem, and disappeared into the massive grove of olive trees. Why? Because He knew His enemies wanted Him dead. He knew they didn't want to arrest Him in the daylight or in full view of the crowd, and He needed a clandestine place where He could hide at night in the darkness with His disciples.

On Tuesday morning, He had one thing in mind. He went directly to the temple and He assaulted its corrupt operations for the second time (Luke 19:45–46). He had done this before at the beginning of His ministry (John 2:13–17). Both times, He identified the whole Jewish religious system as apostate. His first public assault was to expose the vile hypocrisy of the ruling religious elite and declare that divine judgment was coming. He punctuated that message at the close of His earthly ministry by attacking the wicked temple operation again.

The temple operation was corrupt to the core. The scribes and Pharisees were arch-hypocrites and ruthless manipulators. The scribes were the law experts who informed the legalistic religion of the Pharisees. The Pharisees were the purveyors of that religion throughout the synagogue system, which made their works-righteousness the dominant form of Judaism. The Sadducees, another sect of Jews, ran the temple enterprises, which amounted to little more than a sanctimonious scam.

They extorted money out of people by discrediting the sacrifices they had brought, forcing them to buy the animals the Sadducees sold. They cheated people on the exchange of money and even created a means by which the people could buy divine blessing. It was a wholly corrupt system of meritorious works, self-righteousness, and blatant hypocrisy—all of it helping to line the pockets of the religious rulers.

That's why on Tuesday Jesus declared, "It is written, 'And My house shall be a house of prayer,' but you have made it a robbers' den" (Luke 19:46). God's house was intended to be a place of worship, prayer, and communion with the true and living God by the means He had established. They had turned it into a haven for thieves. They were using God's law and His house to extort money from the people and make themselves wealthy. It was false religion in its worst possible form, and Christ did not take lightly their vile abuses. Mark's gospel describes the scene: "And He entered the temple and began to drive out those who were buying and selling in the temple, and overturned the tables of the money changers and the seats of those who were selling doves; and He would not permit anyone to carry merchandise through the temple" (Mark 11:15–16). Jesus spent the rest of that long day interacting with people, healing the sick, and teaching. He then went back to the Mount of Olives and lay on the ground to sleep.

On Wednesday, He returned to Jerusalem. This was the last day Jesus ever taught publicly. He preached about the kingdom and answered several questions from the scribes and Pharisees meant to stump and frustrate Him (Luke 20:1–40).

Wednesday was also His last public confrontation with the religious elite, who feverishly despised Him. Their hatred had been simmering for years, since the beginning of His public ministry when He first disrupted the corrupt temple operation, striking a damaging blow at their desecration. Not only had He disrupted their operation, but He also discredited their integrity and validity. They hated Him because He assaulted their theology, their seats of power, and their fragile truce with Rome. He exposed their false righteousness, and He did not do it subtly. He publicly denounced them. He openly condemned their corruption and their hypocrisy. And they hated Him for His supposed blasphemy, because He claimed to be equal with God—a notion they refused to entertain. Their consuming hatred for Him eventually drove them to plot His murder.

So here at the conclusion of Jesus' public ministry, it's critical to hear what He says. These words in Luke 20:41–21:6 are His final words, His last message to the masses. And what is His last message about? It's about His identity. *Who is Jesus?* He'd been telling them for three years. He'd been telling them day after day. He had made the claims over and over that He was the Messiah, and He verified those claims with undeniable evidence. Here, at the end, He returns to this pivotal issue once again.

Missing the Messiah

Scripture makes it clear that the Jews had high expectations for the long-awaited Messiah—expectations that Christ didn't necessarily meet at first glance. They were sure that the Messiah would be a man—not an angel, and not God, but a man. And not just any man, but a son of David. Based on the promises of God's covenant with David, they looked for David's heir to establish the everlasting kingdom. They expected that when the Messiah came, He would be a man of immense authority and influence who would sweep into power, overthrow the Romans and all the enemies of Israel, and fulfill instantly all the kingdom promises to Abraham, David, and the prophets. In doing those things, He would bring full salvation to Israel.

Even the disciples thought that. Luke tells us they believed the Messiah would bring the kingdom (Acts 1:6). But the people thought He would be *just* a man and a son of David. And our Lord used those expectations to raise the ultimate question: Is the Messiah merely a man?

We can divide these final public statements into categories—let's think of Luke 20:41–44 as Christ's final invitation. In spite of the hatred from the leaders, in spite of the fickle interest by the uncommitted crowds, He was still the compassionate evangelist. Just days away from the agonies of the cross, He would once again clarify who He is and call repentant sinners to believe.

In the parallel account in Matthew 22:42, Jesus asks, "What do you think about the Christ, whose son is He?" He directed His words to the Pharisees and the scribes, but He could be heard by all the people. Matthew 22:42 records their reply: "The son of David." Everyone understood and expected the Messiah's royal lineage. Interestingly, Matthew records the question with a definite article: "What do you think about *the* Christ?" (emphasis added). At that moment Jesus wasn't emphasizing Himself. He was simply asking, "What is your view of the Messiah? Whose son is He?" And they replied, "David's."

That's as much as they understood. They had a fundamentally flawed conception of the Messiah—they expected Him to be nothing more than a man with the inherited right to the throne of Israel. It wasn't overtly heretical or blasphemous, but it was incomplete, and when it comes to the person and work of Christ, incomplete equals wrong.

Any Jew would have answered the question of the Messiah's identity the same way, as that is what the Old Testament taught in 2 Samuel 7, Psalm 89, Ezekiel 37, and a number of other passages. According to Matthew 9:27, "As Jesus went on from there, two blind men followed Him, crying out, 'Have mercy on us, Son of David!'" Luke records in chapter 18 that later on in Jesus' ministry, as He was coming through Jericho, He ran into another blind man. The blind man cried out to Him, "Son of David, have mercy on me!" (Luke 18:39). Matthew 12 reads, "Then a demon-possessed man who was blind and mute was brought to Jesus, and He healed him, so that the mute man spoke and saw. All the crowds were amazed, and were saying, 'This man cannot be the son of David, can he?'" (Matt. 12:22–23). That was what everyone understood: that the Messiah was a son of David.

In fact, Zacharias, the father of John the Baptist, serves as a good illustration in this regard. When Zacharias heard that the coming of the Messiah was imminent (because God promised to give him and his barren wife, Elizabeth, a child who would be the forerunner of the Messiah), he was filled with the Holy Spirit (Luke 1:67) and prophesied,

> Blessed be the Lord God of Israel,
> For He has visited us and accomplished redemption
>   for His people,
> And has raised up a horn of salvation for us
> In the house of David His servant. (vv. 68–69)

Since the Messiah was to be the son of David, the most obvious way for the Jewish leaders to discredit Jesus or disprove His claims of messiahship would have been to pull out the temple records and show that He was not born in the line of David. You can be certain that the Pharisees and scribes researched and confirmed that crucial detail. Further, the Messiah had to come before the temple was destroyed, because all the records were destroyed as well. Those genealogies and the unassailable lineage of Christ stand as testaments to the precision of God's sovereign plan.

With that said, the Pharisees' answer to Christ's question is accurate: He *is* David's son. But their answer is inadequate and incomplete. For the rest of the answer, the Lord gave a brief exposition from the Old Testament.

> How is it that they say the Christ is David's son? For David himself says in the book of Psalms,
> "The Lord said to my Lord,
> 'Sit at my right hand,

Until I make Your enemies a footstool for Your feet.'"
Therefore David calls Him 'Lord,' and how is He his
son?" (Luke 20:41–44).

This is absolutely stunning and brilliant. No self-respecting
father would ever call his son "Lord." Why is David calling his
son "Lord," *Adonai*, in Psalm 110:1?

Some Jewish commentators have concluded that David
made a mistake, as though David shouldn't have said that. But
Matthew 22:43 says, "Then how does David in the Spirit call
Him 'Lord'?" Other critics have suggested that David spoke
this in his own human spirit. But Mark 12:36 says, "David
himself said in the Holy Spirit." When David called the Messiah his Lord, it was by the Holy Spirit's inspiration.

Psalm 110 is a messianic psalm, and it was always inter-
preted by the Jews as messianic until the early church period.
It's the psalm most often quoted by New Testament writers.
The way Jesus used this psalm verifies its messianic character,
its Davidic authorship, and His own deity. This psalm was such
a persuasive proof of Jesus' messianic claims that for hundreds
of years, the Jews abandoned the historic interpretation. They
applied it to Abraham, Melchizedek, and even Judas Mac-
cabeus. It has been relentlessly attacked by rabbis and critics
who want to reject its prophetic element, its Davidic authorship, and, ultimately, the deity of Jesus Christ.

Jesus said David wrote it, and that he wrote it by the Holy
Spirit. Further, He said that David was prophesying concern-
ing Him, the Messiah, and that the Messiah is David's Lord.

And what did God say to David's Lord in Psalm 110:1? "Sit at My right hand until I make Your enemies a footstool for Your feet." Putting the Messiah at God's right hand is putting Him in a position of equality. The right hand is the symbol of God's power. He invests into His Son, the Messiah, all power and all authority, and we hear that repeated in the New Testament. The Messiah will not only be David's son humanly, He will be David's Lord divinely. He is the son of David and the Son of God, David's son *and* David's Lord. "And we saw His glory," John writes, "glory as of the only begotten from the Father, full of grace and truth" (John 1:14).

This is the only true explanation for Jesus—the *only* one. He showed His divine ability to create, He shared omnipotence with God the Father, He commanded the elements, He commanded all creatures, He created food, He created healthy bodies, He raised the dead, He forgave sin, and He pronounced judgment—all elements of divine omnipotence. He had the attribute of omnipresence and was able to be everywhere at all times if He desired to be (John 1:48). He was omniscient. He knew everything that was in the heart of man so that no one needed to tell Him anything about a man (John 2:24–25). Therefore, He shared the infinite knowledge of God. He was immutable. He is the same today, yesterday, and forever: always holy, true, wise, sovereign, loving, eternal, glorious, and unchanging. He accepted worship. He is to be sought in prayer. In every sense, He is God. He even shared some of the same titles with God: rock, stumbling stone, Savior, Redeemer, Holy One, Lord of Hosts, King, and First and Last.

When we look at the life of Jesus Christ, we're not surprised to see manifestly that He is God. If God became man, we would expect His human life to be sinless. His was. If God, the holy true God, became man, we would expect Him to live in perfect righteousness. He did. If God became man, we would expect His words to be the greatest words ever spoken. They were. If God became man, we would expect Him to exert a profound, unequaled power over humanity. He did. If God became man, we would expect supernatural demonstrations. There were many. If God became man, we would expect Him to manifest the love of God. He did. There's no other possible conclusion: Jesus is David's Son, who is *also* David's Lord.

Matthew adds a sober footnote to this scene in 22:46: "No one was able to answer Him a word, nor did anyone dare from that day on to ask Him another question." Sadly, it doesn't say they repented and believed. Instead, we can assume they just ramped up the hatred, further hardening their hearts against the truth and deepening their resolve to see Christ silenced. They rejected Christ's final invitation—their last opportunity to bend the knee and acknowledge that He is God as well as man, David's son and David's Lord.

It was in that moment that the final invitation ended for that generation in Israel.

Condemning Corruption

In spite of three years of abundant proof of His divine nature, Israel sided against the Lord Jesus with His enemies. With His final public words, Jesus issued a stern warning to the Jews about their religious leaders and the spiritual threat they posed to Israel. Think of it as His final condemnation on their blasphemous apostasy. "Beware of the scribes, who like to walk around in long robes, and love respectful greetings in the marketplaces, and chief seats in the synagogues and places of honor at banquets, who devour widows' houses, and for appearance's sake offer long prayers. These will receive greater condemnation" (Luke 20:46–47).

Right in the shadow of the temple, Jesus pronounced a severe and stunning damnation on apostate Judaism. It's a blistering, scathing rebuke aimed at the false religion of the priests and Pharisees. Luke gives us two verses in this exchange, but Matthew 23 gives us the whole malediction. Jesus repeatedly condemns them as hypocrites, and pronounces severe woes against them for their abusive practices. He walked out of the temple after having cursed the religious leaders of Israel and warned the people, "You're going down with them if you don't get away from them."

Jesus' condemnation of the religious leaders is very focused. He talks about their hypocritical attitude—they like to walk around in long robes, love greetings and chief seats, and are proud, self-serving, and self-righteous. But there's only one sinful act mentioned here: they "devour widows' houses" (Luke 20:47). This is the only specific sin of action, rendered in the Greek as *katesthiō*, which means to "consume," "plunder," or "eat up." How bad was this religion? It had descended to the

16

point that those in charge were getting rich by the abuse of the most defenseless people. That's how corrupt the first-century practice of Judaism was and how far it had strayed from the heart of God.

Throughout the whole Old Testament, in various covenants and in the law, God repeatedly made provisions to care for the poor. That same focus continued into the New Testament. James 1:27 says, "Pure and undefiled religion in the sight of our God and Father is this: to visit orphans and widows in their distress." This is the heart of God—tender compassion, particularly for those who need it most.

With that in mind, Christ was condemning not only their theological apostasy, but also their practical apostasy. Their spiritual defection led them to become isolated, self-serving spiritual hypocrites who were getting fatter and richer, building a religious empire on the backs of the most beleaguered, defeated, and defenseless. According to their religion, if someone was a widow, there had to have been sin in her life, for which she was being punished by God. Women in that era were second-class citizens to begin with. Being a widow made one the lowest of the low, and it gave the religious elite license to treat her with disdain. Publicly, the elites made a show of their piety and devotion, while privately they devoured the resources of the very ones they were responsible to provide for and protect. They were blasphemous frauds, and they would soon receive a severe judgment for their treacherous behavior.

A Tragic Illustration

The events described in the next passage ought to shake us. Luke begins chapter 21 by noting that "Jesus looked up." What does that tell you? Simply that Jesus had been looking down.

If we put together the whole picture presented across the Synoptic Gospels, we see that Jesus was understandably weary. It had been a long, exhausting week. He had just delivered the fierce diatribe recorded in Matthew 23 and had been pulled at and pushed by the crowd all day. He was tired. His heart was grieved, as it had been since He came into the city on Monday, when the mere sight of Jerusalem caused Him to weep (Luke 19:41). He was brokenhearted. He had assaulted the temple operation the day before and had just issued a final, urgent warning against the lies of the religious elite and their corrupt system.

But He also knew it wouldn't make a difference—in less than two days, the fickle crowd would be crying out for His blood. In spite of everything He had said and done, most of the people He had ministered and preached to would follow their leaders on the broad road that leads to hell.

Mark 12:41 tells us that He found a place to sit in the area of the temple treasury, which was in the Women's Court. He taught there because it was a large open space where men, women, and even Gentiles could gather to hear Him. It was the same part of the temple where the thirteen trumpet-shaped receptacles were located—where the people and the Pharisees came to deposit their offering money publicly. This is what the system demanded—redemption was purchased by giving alms.

In Matthew 6, Christ said that people had trumpets blown to announce their arrival, putting their philanthropy on display. He watched the rich putting their gifts into the treasury, and according to Mark 12:41, they put in large amounts.

And then Jesus saw a poor widow putting in two small copper coins. The coin was called a lepton. It was equal to 1/132 of a denarius, and it was the smallest currency the Jews used. In moments, Jesus would leave the city with His disciples. He was surrounded by this magnificent Herodian temple—which had been under construction for fifty years—the gleaming, ornate symbol of this rich religion. But before they walked out, Jesus noticed this widow and said to His disciples, "Truly I say to you, this poor widow put in more than all of them; for they all out of their surplus put into the offering; but she out of her poverty put in all she had to live on" (Luke 21:3–4).

How many sermons and exhortations have you heard regarding this story—often immediately followed by an offering? They say, "O Lord, may we learn from the widow!" But what's really going on here? If you want to argue that this brief episode is about giving, then the principle you must draw from the text is that God wants us to give absolutely everything we have and go home to die. Because that is what she did. The text says, "She put in all she had to live on" (v. 4). The Greek literally says, "She put in all her life." There was nothing left for her to live on. In all likelihood, she would soon starve to death or die of exposure. Jesus was essentially saying, "The people who have more, they give out of their surplus. When she's done giving, she's got nothing left." So, if this is a lesson on giving, the only lesson we can take from it is to give everything and go home, and hope someone comes to your door with more, or else you'll die. That can't be a biblical mandate.

Others might argue, "No, the lesson here is she had a really good attitude." Yet Scripture doesn't say a word about her attitude—it simply tells us what she did. All we know is that she was a destitute widow who gave far more relative to everyone else, because she gave 100 percent. We can't arbitrarily add in imaginary elements to make this vignette an exhortation to give cheerfully.

In fact, this familiar story has been twisted and contorted all sorts of ways to wrench out of it some principle about selflessness, humility, and sacrificial giving. But there is no principle for giving here. All those ideas are imposed on the narrative. That becomes clear the moment you consider the context of Christ's words. He's just been proclaiming judgment and condemnation against the scribes and Pharisees. We must not assume that seeing this woman give her meager gift would so radically break His train of thought that He would abruptly launch into a quick treatise for believers on sacrificial giving.

The disciples' reaction also confirms that this was not a divine statement on giving to the church. None of them asks Him to clarify or expand on His point—to help them understand if He really wanted them to surrender all their earthly belongings and follow this woman into abject poverty. No one bothers to ask if Jesus is really instructing them to give to the degree that it makes them a burden for other people to support.

They knew that Christ wasn't commending her gift. He didn't say He was proud of her or that she had a good heart. Instead, He was saying: "Judaism is so corrupt, it devours widows' houses, and here's an illustration. This poor woman is so deceived by the notion that she could gain God's favor by giving up all her money that she'll give her last cents." Therefore, what we have here is the Lord's condemnation of anyone who would manipulate His Word and name to deceive people so as to line their pockets. Jesus unequivocally pronounced damnation on any religionist who builds a personal fortune on the backs of the destitute and the desperate with promises of divine favor leading to success, prosperity, health, and wealth. This poor woman's gift stands as a testament to the abusive perversions of such false religion.

As Jesus and the disciples walk away, the Lord turns around and looks at the temple, glistening in the late afternoon in Jerusalem. While the disciples discussed its beautiful and expensive adornment, He says, "As for these things which you are looking at, the days will come in which there will not be left one stone upon another which will not be torn down" (Luke 21:6). Not only would the individual scribes and Pharisees face a greater condemnation for their abuses, but soon the entire religious system would come crumbling down. Just forty years later, Jerusalem and the temple were flattened, all the genealogical records were destroyed, and the sacrificial system came to an end. The imminent demise of the Jewish religious system made Israel's allegiance to it—and the woman's misdirected offering—all the more heartbreaking.

A Final Question

As we come to the end of Passion Week, in the hours before Christ's arrest and trial, we have to ask, is this a bad ending? Is this any way for the story of the Son of God to end—rejected, betrayed, heartbroken, and arrested? And does this apparent failure in any way damage or discredit Christ's divine claims? Was Jesus, in the end, just a man with extraordinary insights on morality and religion?

No. And Luke 22 shows us why.

The chapter begins with the plotting of the chief priests and scribes. After the fierce and public rebuke they received in Matthew 23, their fury with Christ reaches new heights. They are now more determined than ever to silence Him, and they finally have an insider to help. Luke 22:3 tells us, "Satan entered into Judas." He knew exactly where Jesus would be on the Mount of Olives, and he worked out a deal with the chief priests to lead them to Gethsemane, where they would finally have the Lord in their clutches.

It's now Thursday night. Jesus and His disciples are in the upper room, celebrating the last legitimate Passover. It's here that Christ institutes the Lord's Supper and warns His friends that their futures will not be easy. He tells them about the persecution and hatred they will face from the world (John 15–16). And then He makes a stunning statement. In the intimacy of the upper room, Jesus makes the staggering claim that He is the One prophesied in Isaiah 53: "For I tell you that this which is written must be fulfilled in Me, 'And He was numbered with the transgressors'; for that which refers to Me has its fulfill-ment" (Luke 22:37).

Israel rejected Christ's final invitation and ignored His final condemnation—let's call this the final realization. Jesus quotes Isaiah 53:12, not in order to isolate that one verse, but to bring into focus the entire chapter. Twice He says, "That which is written must be fulfilled in Me," both at the beginning and at the end of Luke 22:37.

He's asserting that His ministry—and soon, His life—is not a failure. It had to be this way. The wicked machinations of Israel's apostate system were not a defeat. The worst they could do was going to fulfill the plan of God. As Luke would write in the sequel to his gospel, "This Man, delivered over by the predetermined plan and foreknowledge of God, you nailed to a cross by the hands of godless men and put Him to death" (Acts 2:23).

Jesus is God's Lamb. It was not Judas' betrayal, the chief priests' plot, Pilate's indifference, or even Satan's schemes that ultimately put Christ on the cross. It was God's plan all along. Why? Because someone had to take the place of sinners. According to Old Testament prophecy, He had to be "num-bered with the transgressors" (Isa. 53:12). This wasn't a final, heartbreaking defeat. This was necessary fulfillment of what He came to do. He had told His disciples: "I have a baptism to undergo, and how distressed I am until it is accomplished!" (Luke 12:50).

Now He is saying unmistakably, "I am the fulfillment of Isaiah 53." He specifically identifies one line: "numbered with the transgressors" (v. 12). But that line is only one of twenty in that chapter that speak of His substitutionary identification with sinners.

We can take a look at Isaiah 53 and see it divides into four parts. The first section actually begins in 52:14, where Isaiah describes the *suffering* substitute:

Just as many were astonished at you, My people,
So His appearance was marred more than any man
And His form more than the sons of men.

Isaiah 53:2 continues the theme:

He has no stately form or majesty
That we should look upon Him,
Nor appearance that we should be attracted to Him.

He would be scarred, disfigured, and repulsive to onlookers. From there, the prophet moves to a second emphasis: the *sufficient* substitute. Isaiah writes:

Surely our griefs He Himself bore,
And our sorrows He carried;
Yet we ourselves esteemed Him stricken,
Smitten of God, and afflicted.
But He was pierced through for our transgressions,
He was crushed for our iniquities;
The chastening for our well-being fell upon Him,

And by His scourging we are healed.
All of us like sheep have gone astray,
Each of us has turned to his own way;
But the LORD has caused the iniquity of us all
To fall on Him. (Isa. 53:4–6)

As our sufficient substitute, Christ paid the penalty of our transgressions. He has taken the punishment of our iniquities. Our guilt and the wrath it demanded fell on Him instead. He is the only sufficient substitute—the only One who could stand in our place and shoulder the weight of our sin.

In verses 7–9, Isaiah further describes Him as the *submissive* substitute:

He was oppressed and He was afflicted,
Yet He did not open His mouth;
Like a lamb that is led to slaughter,
And like a sheep that is silent before its shearers,
So He did not open His mouth.
By oppression and judgment He was taken away;
And as for His generation, who considered
That He was cut off out of the land of the living
For the transgression of my people, to whom the
    stroke was due?
His grave was assigned with wicked men,
Yet He was with a rich man in His death,
Because He had done no violence,
Nor was there any deceit in His mouth.

Almighty God took on the penalty of our sin, along with all the hatred, mockery, and abuse the world could sling at Him—all without a thought for His own self-defense. Christ willingly submitted to the horrors of the cross for our sake.

Isaiah 53 closes with a final perspective on Christ's sacrifice—the prophet introduces us to the *sovereign* substitute in verses 10–12:

> But the LORD was pleased
> To crush Him, putting Him to grief;
> If He would render Himself as a guilt offering,
> He will see His offspring,
> He will prolong His days,
> And the good pleasure of the LORD will prosper in
>   His hand.
> As a result of the anguish of His soul,
> He will see it and be satisfied;
> By His knowledge the Righteous One,
> My Servant, will justify the many,
> As He will bear their iniquities.
> Therefore, I will allot Him a portion with the great,
> And He will divide the booty with the strong;
> Because He poured out Himself to death,
> And was numbered with the transgressors;
> Yet He Himself bore the sin of many,
> And interceded for the transgressors.
> (Isa. 53:10–12)

In the end, this suffering, sufficient, submissive substitute was the One who "poured out Himself to death." The Messiah couldn't simply be a man, because no man was fit to bear the sins of the world, no man could accept such vicious scorn without reprisal, and no man could pour himself out as a guilt offering. By identifying Himself as the One who would be "numbered with the transgressors," Jesus wasn't only claiming to be the Messiah—He was identifying as God's Lamb, providing the substitutionary sacrifice for sinners that opened the grace of God for forgiveness and eternal life.

Do you want to know the most stunning and most overlooked fact about Isaiah 53? The verbs are in the past tense. Here is a prophet who was writing hundreds of years before the cross but who was looking back at it. And the prophet writes, "He *bore*, He *was* smitten of God, He *was* pierced, He *was* scourged, He *was* oppressed, He *was* afflicted," all in the past tense. Why is that? This magnificent chapter is written from the perspective of that great day, still in the prophetic future, when "all Israel will be saved" (Rom. 11:26). Then the Jewish people will look back on the cross. And they will see the truth.

What does Zechariah 12:10 say? "They will look on Me whom they have pierced; and they will mourn for Him." The end result of Israel's rejection of Christ as Messiah in the future is the salvation of Israel. Jesus culminates His life and His public ministry by telling apostate Israel, "If you reject me, you are damned." Then He pulls His disciples aside and explains that their rejection isn't a final failure; it's a necessary element for the fulfillment of Isaiah 53. More than that, Jews will one day look back at the cross and find the promised salvation of Isaiah 53. The cross is not defeat—it is the victorious purpose for which He came in the first place.

The glorious realities of our Christ are like the numberless stars of heaven. Each feature of His life shines with blazing brilliance, and there are so many they're almost incalculable. We've just picked out a little glimpse of His majesty and His glory. We love our Christ, but we can only love Him because He first loved us. May God forgive us for our cold and indifferent hearts, and may we grow to love the Lord Jesus with all our heart, soul, mind, and strength. What a privilege that we should be among those who look back and get the story right. May we thank God for this grace, and may we give Him all the glory.

Chapter Two

JESUS IS HOLY

C hrist's holiness is an inexhaustible theme—its height, depth, and breadth will fill our perfected wonder someday. This theme will occupy both our holy fascination and our eternal curiosity. A story is told of a little boy who was visiting the Atlantic Ocean for the first time. He took a little bottle and filled it with ocean water to take back home to Kansas and show his friends the ocean. Similarly, as we consider the grand theme of the holiness of Christ, I will attempt to show my little bottle. But where in Scripture shall we go to fill it and display the holiness of Christ?

We could turn to Luke 1 and Gabriel's announcement to Mary that she would have a holy offspring. We could go to the testimony of God the Father at the baptism of Jesus, when the Father affirmed the holiness of Christ by saying, "You are My beloved Son, in You I am well-pleased" (Luke 3:22). We could consider the testimony of the Holy Spirit, when He descended

GOOD NEWS

upon Jesus, affirming the perfect union and agreement within the Trinity. We could consider Jesus' testimony to His own holiness when He confessed that He and the Father are one (John 10:30). We could survey the Epistles of the New Testament and hear their writers testify—through the inspiration of the Holy Spirit—to the deity of Jesus Christ, and consequently, His holiness. And we could certainly go to the book of Hebrews, where we find the Holy Spirit repeatedly exalts and extolls the holiness of Christ.

Further still, we could look at accounts of the resurrection and the ascension, which are divine affirmations of Christ's divine perfection. And finally, we could go to the transfiguration, where we actually see the unveiled holiness of Christ—a moment in which He is revealed without human limitations. As we consider the many places in Scripture that reveal the holiness of Christ, the transfiguration initially stands out as a wonderful text to explore, but it's such a brief glimpse.

Instead, let's look somewhere that offers us an extended view—a fuller picture of the unveiled, holy glory of Christ. I believe the first chapter of Revelation is where we find the best water to fill our little bottles with a vision of the holiness of Christ.

Why Does Christ's Holiness Matter?

This first chapter of Revelation certainly contains the most profoundly transcendent picture of Christ in His glory and holiness. And yet, as profound and transcendent as it is, it's also intensely practical for believers. The church is called to be the all-beautiful bride of Christ. She often appears, however, more like a ragged Cinderella for whom the clock has struck midnight.

As a pastor, I am burdened for the church. I long for people to experience deep, rich communion with the living Christ. I desire that they would have power over temptation and sin and live triumphantly. I long for them to passionately pursue holiness and purity and submit to the authority of the Word of God. And I trust that other pastors have the same desires for their congregations.

Furthermore, I desire that there might be godly, faithful pastors to shepherd and protect the church. Many Christians have these same desires as they look at the church today. I want to protect God's people from hirelings and deceivers, so I spend a lot of time watching and warning the church.

Most of all, I long for the people of God to reflect the glory of Christ. The church, after all, is not only Christ's bride; it is also His herald and representative on earth—the instrument by which the Lord takes the gospel to the whole world. I long for the body of Christ to be salt and light in a world that desperately needs both.

Those are the things I, and many Christians, want for the church. And while we look at the church with these compelling desires, in reality, they seem so far away. It seems that the church is often adrift, miles from where it should be and without the means to right the ship. It is easy to be discouraged.

But in Revelation 1, in John's vision of the glorious Christ, I find great encouragement. When this vision came to John, it wasn't particularly encouraging, as we'll see. But as we look back at this text of Scripture from our vantage point, we find great comfort. Christ's holiness matters because it lifts our eyes above the sorry state of the church and helps us focus on His glory and greatness. In Revelation 1, through John's eyes, we see our holy Christ manifesting Himself in transcendent glory in the midst of His church.

Consider the Source

But first, let's reacquaint ourselves with John, the human author of Revelation. He was living in exile on the island of Patmos at the time of this vision. Five miles wide at its widest point and ten miles long, Patmos is essentially a rock in the Mediterranean. It's about forty miles from Miletus, the coastal city connected to Ephesus, where John had apparently ministered later in his life.

Writing sometime around AD 96, John was an old man. His life was nearly over. His friends, the Apostles, were long gone, most of them having been martyred, systematically terminated by the Christ-haters. He had lived to see Jerusalem sacked and the temple destroyed by the Romans. Under the leadership of Titus Vespasian, Rome slaughtered as many as a million Jews and destroyed hundreds of towns and villages throughout Israel. John had lived long enough to see all those horrors and more, and he no doubt harbored little hope of seeing Christ's return in his lifetime.

In fact, we can assume that—at least on a human level—little of the exciting, enthusiastic, exhilarating hope that had burned in John's heart during Christ's life and the early days of the church remained at this point. He was in his nineties, forced to live out the rest of his days as a criminal, doomed to die in exile. And on top of everything else, any hopes for a future kingdom of Israel had been dashed, and the church wasn't doing well either.

John likely ministered in the churches in Asia Minor for a time—the same churches addressed in chapters 2 and 3 of Revelation. He must have known that Ephesus had left its first love, that Pergamum was idolatrous and immoral, that Thyatira was compromised with sin and worldliness, that Laodicea was lukewarm and apathetic, and that Sardis was just plain dead. Far worse than his brutal circumstance was the knowledge that these churches were in horrifying disarray. It is a bleak picture, and it reveals a man desperately in need of comfort and some word of hope for the future.

In some ways, we can identify with John. Today, we see too many churches like Ephesus that have abandoned their first love. We see idolatrous and immoral churches like Pergamum. We see churches like Thyatira, caught in the snare of worldliness. We see churches consumed by nauseating apathy like Laodicea. And we see dead churches like Sardis. Whether it's liberalism, legalism, heresy, man-centeredness, carnality, apathy, or materialism, we see it in the church today. We ache for the church. Like John, we need to see a vision to assure us of what Christ is doing in His church.

And that's what we find in Revelation 1. In verse 9, John

begins by saying, "I, John, your brother and fellow partaker in the tribulation and kingdom and perseverance which are in Jesus, was on the island called Patmos because of the word of God and the testimony of Jesus." He refers to himself as "I, John, your brother and fellow partaker," indicating that he saw himself as equal to everyone else.

In verse 10, he says, "I was in the Spirit." What does that mean? In simple terms, it means that he was receiving supernatural revelation, most likely via a vision. He was perceiving and experiencing something beyond his normal human senses and apprehension. Under the control of the Holy Spirit, he transcended the limits of human understanding and was brought into a supernatural plane of experience to receive specific, direct revelation from the Lord.

He also tells us it happened "on the Lord's Day." We shouldn't misconstrue this as an eschatological reference to the day of the Lord. Since the second century, the church has almost universally referred to Sunday as the Lord's Day, and we have every reason to believe that that's what John means here. He's simply saying it was a Sunday on Patmos.

And on that particular Sunday, God lifted John beyond his human senses and spoke to him. "I heard behind me a loud voice like the sound of a trumpet, saying, 'Write in a book what you see, and send it to the seven churches: to Ephesus and to Smyrna and to Pergamum and to Thyatira and to Sardis and to Philadelphia and to Laodicea'" (Rev. 1:10–11). Of those seven, only Smyrna and Philadelphia were not rebuked by the Lord. The rest received serious and severe indictments. It is important to note that these seven cities were the postal centers of Asia Minor. In fact, they are listed in sequence, starting with Ephesus. This was the ancient postal route, operating in the order indicated in verse 11.

In verse 12, we read, "Then I turned to see the voice that was speaking with me. And having turned I saw seven golden lampstands." These golden lampstands represent the seven churches the Lord mentioned by name. But they also serve as representatives of all churches throughout church history. Biblically, the number seven represents completeness, and that's what we have here—a comprehensive picture of the church in all its variations. The lampstands themselves were nothing out of the ordinary—just a tall rod with a sturdy base and a platform to support an oil lamp. That they were made of gold speaks of their precious value in the eyes of the Lord. Most important, though, was their function. With the wick lit in the oil-filled dish, it provided obvious and unmistakable light. Just as these lampstands were used to illuminate a room, Christ had called the church to be the light of the world (Matt. 5:14–16).

For our purposes, the most important aspect of John's vision is found in Revelation 1:13. John writes, "In the middle of the lampstands I saw one like a son of man." John turns to hear the voice, and as he looks, he sees the unveiled Christ in holy glory, standing in the midst of His church.

Sometimes, we may feel as though the Lord has abandoned His church. John may have felt the same way. He may have wondered what was going on in Israel, and if God's plans for the church had been thwarted somehow. I think similar thoughts were on Isaiah's mind when he received all the revelations of woe against Israel. Knowing that God was going to send a great army to destroy Israel, Isaiah might have gone to the temple simply to make sure God was still on His throne. There, he had a vision (Isa. 6). And as Isaiah's vision began, he immediately saw the Lord high and lifted up. Without a doubt, God was still there. What we need to see—and what John needed to see in exile on Patmos—is that in spite of the disarray and chaos of the church, Christ is still in her midst. And as this simple vision unfolds, it provides us with some profound reassurance about the nature and character of Christ.

Holy Presence

John's vision in Revelation 1 reveals several aspects of Christ's holiness. The first is His holy presence.

In verse 13, John writes, "In the middle of the lampstands I saw one like a son of man." This magnificent term "son of man" is a messianic term borrowed from the book of Daniel. It speaks to the incarnation, identifying God as man in human flesh. Daniel speaks of the Messiah as "One like a Son of Man" who is given "dominion, glory and a kingdom, that all the peoples, nations and men of every language might serve Him" (Dan. 7:13–14). The text goes on to say "His dominion is an everlasting dominion" and His kingdom will never be destroyed.

Now here in Revelation, we see Christ in His kingdom, moving in His church. It is *His* church, bestowed on Him by the Father as a love gift. The church is the bride of the Son of

God, purchased with His own blood, and guaranteed for eternity. John's gospel testifies to this truth with these words from Christ: "All that the Father gives Me will come to me. . . . Of all that He has given Me I lose nothing, but raise it up on the last day" (John 6:37, 39).

In his vision, John turns to identify whose voice he's hearing, and he sees the holy presence of Christ in His church. We should rest assured that He is always there. The Lord of the church has unceasing communion with His people. The true church lives in unbroken communion with its Savior.

This is a vital truth, but Christians today seem to have trouble keeping it in view. Perhaps you've heard someone say, "So-and-so is out of fellowship with the Lord." Such a statement reflects careless thinking. The term *fellowship* (Greek *koinōnia*) means "partnership" or "communion," and neither our communion nor our partnership with the Lord is subject to change. Our union with Christ can't be altered. It's eternal. No matter how weak they are, no matter how vacillating, no matter how sinful, God's true people maintain an eternal and permanent relationship with Him, and the life of God is in them forever.

That's why, in Matthew 28:20, Jesus said, "And lo, I am with you always," and in Matthew 18:20, "I am there in their midst." John 14:18 makes clear, "I will not leave you as orphans; I will come to you." And Jesus says in John 14:23, "If anyone loves Me . . . My Father will love him, and We will come to him and make Our abode with him." Hebrews 13:5 reinforces this truth by quoting Christ as saying, "I will never desert you, nor will I ever forsake you." You may at times lose the joy of your salvation. But no matter how difficult the circumstances or devastating the failures, you will never be out of fellowship with the living Christ.

The same goes for His church. No matter how the church struggles, the living Lord is alive and always working in its midst. He never abandons His true disciples. The fellowship never stops. It is unbreakable and eternal. And the One who chose us, justified us, and sanctifies us will one day glorify us. Christ's unfailing presence in His church, working and moving among His people, ought to be a tremendous encouragement to us.

Holy Intercession

The second aspect of Christ's holiness that we notice in John's vision is the holy intercession of Christ. In his vision, John sees Jesus clothed in a robe that reaches to His feet, with a golden belt or sash across His chest (Rev. 1:13). You might initially think of these heavenly garments as arbitrary details, but they depict a glorious truth about our Lord. The outfit John describes is the same one worn by Israel's high priest. The picture he's painting is unmistakable—not only is Christ communing with His church, He is interceding on behalf of His church as our Great High Priest.

The book of Hebrews speaks of Jesus' High Priestly ministry in a number of places. Hebrews 2:17–18 tells us that He is "a merciful and faithful high priest," able to come to the aid of those who are tempted. Hebrews 3:1 calls Jesus the "High Priest of our confession." A wonderful passage in Hebrews 4:15 tells us that Jesus is a High Priest who can sympathize with our weaknesses. He was "tempted in all things as we are, yet without sin." He is holy, innocent, and undefiled (Heb. 7:26).

Hebrews 9:11–12 describes Christ's superiority over all other high priests: "But when Christ appeared as a high priest of the good things to come, He entered through the greater and more perfect tabernacle, not made with hands, that is to say, not of this creation; and not through the blood of goats and calves, but through His own blood, He entered the holy place once for all, having obtained eternal redemption." As our High Priest, Christ offered the only perfect and acceptable sacrifice for our sins: Himself.

And as Paul writes in Romans 8, our Lord's work as High Priest continues to this day: "Who will bring a charge against God's elect? God is the one who justifies; who is the one who condemns? Christ Jesus is He who died, yes, rather who was raised, who is at the right hand of God, who also intercedes for us" (vv. 33–34). The Apostle goes on to explain how nothing can assault or alter our relationship with God—because of Christ's intercessory work, we cannot be separated from His love (vv. 38–39).

Even our own sin cannot sever our relationship with Christ. It may cost us some of our eternal reward—John himself warns all believers, saying, "Watch yourselves, that you do not lose what we have accomplished, but that you may receive a full reward" (2 John 8). Sin will cause our crowns to diminish. But nothing can separate us from God, because Christ is always there, interceding on our behalf, pointing back to His completed work on the cross for us.

Holy Purification

In Revelation 1:14–15, we see another aspect of Christ's holy character—we'll call it His holy purification. John describes the scene: "His head and His hair were white like white wool, like snow; and His eyes were like a flame of fire. His feet were like burnished bronze." John is now seeing beyond the clothing described in verse 13 to Christ's glorified physical features, and no detail is incidental.

The description in verse 14—"His head and His hair were white like white wool, like snow"—echoes Daniel 7:9, where the prophet used the same imagery to describe Almighty God on His throne. The point is unmistakable. Jesus is, in fact, Holy God. And the details of their shared appearance illustrate their holiness and purity. The Greek word for "white" in this passage is not like the flat white we might see painted on a wall. It's the word *leukon*, which means "dazzling, blazing, brilliant." It's the bright, gleaming white of light. It's radiant. Through spiritual eyes, John sees the dazzling, blazing, holy character of God manifested in the face of Jesus.

And out of that divine purity comes eyes like a flame of fire. This is another callback to Daniel's vision of God and what he described as eyes "like flaming torches" (Dan. 10:6). In both instances, it's an illustration of God's penetrating, holy omniscience—a physical manifestation of His divine knowledge. What the Lord sees, He sees penetratingly. He sees to its infinite depth. There are no secrets. "And there is no creature hidden from His sight," Hebrews 4:13 says, "but all things are open and laid bare to the eyes of Him with whom we have to do."

We've already seen that Christ intercedes on behalf of His church and that He will not allow them to be separated or condemned. But that does not mean He is not concerned about their holiness. Though they enjoy a present and continuing fellowship with Christ, and though they enjoy His present intercession, which secures their salvation forever, they are also subject to present discipline. Hebrews 12:6 tells us, "For those whom the Lord loves He disciplines,and He scourges every son whom He receives." He wants His bride to be a "pure virgin" (2 Cor. 11:2). He wants His church to be holy and blameless, "having no spot or wrinkle" (Eph. 5:27). He wants His people to be above reproach.

In fact, Christ Himself gave us a prescription for maintaining the purity of the church in Matthew 18—a prescription that, tragically, the church has largely failed to follow. In verses 15–18, we read that if a brother is in sin, we are to go and gently confront him in private. If the person does not repent, we take one or two with us and make another appeal to his conscience. If the sinning brother still does not repent, we tell the whole church. And if he continues in this unrepentant state, we put this person out of the church altogether.

It's often a difficult and painful process. But as hard as it is, we have confidence that the Lord is in our midst as the One ultimately performing the action. That is why He says in Matthew 18:20, "For where two or three have gathered together in My name, I am there in their midst." Many have misconstrued this verse as a promise that a quorum of Christians in any given place can summon God's presence. But this verse isn't talking about God's presence with His people. It's talking about discipline. The point is, when we're involved in confronting sin in the church, the Lord is there, too. He's in our midst as a fellow witness participating in the discipline process, purging and purifying His church.

Christ desires the church's purity so much that there may be times when He takes someone's life. Paul notes that the abuse of the Lord's Table in Corinth had led to some serious consequences for the believers there: "For this reason many among you are weak and sick, and a number sleep [have died]" (1 Cor. 11:30). Ananias and Sapphira were struck down on the spot for lying to God and to the church (Acts 5:1–11). Christ described this zeal for purity to His disciples in John 15:2: "Every branch in Me that does not bear fruit, He takes away; and every branch that bears fruit, He prunes it so that it may bear more fruit." Here is the promise that Christ will aggressively protect the purity and productivity of His people. Some He will prune to maintain and enhance their usefulness; others He will cut off altogether for the sake of the rest of the church.

We work hard to guard the purity of the church, but we can't see everything. John's vision in Revelation 1 reminds us that there is One who sees everything. He's the Lord of the church, and He fiercely protects the purity of His people. That alone ought to give us a vivid glimpse of Christ's holiness.

As the vision continues, the picture becomes a little frightening in verse 15. Jesus' feet are pictured as "burnished bronze"—red-hot, glowing brass. He's moving through His church, and not with fuzzy wool slippers. He's moving through His church with flaming, burning, bronze feet.

The feet of a monarch were always elevated. Usually a king would sit on an elevated throne, putting anyone under his judgment below his feet as a physical depiction of his authority over them. John's vision takes it a step further, picturing Christ's authority along with His power to crush, the power to wound, the power to injure. Such imagery ought to conjure an appropriate fear in us. The Lord is moving through His church. Not only does His holy, penetrating gaze see everything, but He brings down His burning feet in judgment on sin wherever He finds it.

Holy Authority

The feet of burnished bronze are followed by a voice "like the sound of many waters" (Rev. 1:15). On the island prison of Patmos, John would have frequently heard the sound of water. On Patmos, there is no soothing tide washing over the sand. In fact, there's no beach on the island at all—it's just rocks and water. And when the storms come, the water crashes and slaps against the rocks. John would have been well acquainted with the sound of water.

But John isn't using this imagery just because it was the first illustration he could think of. Again, he's intentionally identifying Christ as God. The description of Christ's voice here is the same as the voice of God in Ezekiel 43:2 ("His voice was like the sound of many waters; and the earth shone with His glory"). The Father and the Son speak in the same voice of holy authority over the church. At the transfiguration, God said, "This is My Son, My Chosen One; listen to Him!" (Luke 9:35). We must listen to the Lord Jesus Christ and submit to His authority. "My sheep hear My voice, and I know them, and they follow Me" (John 10:27). In the upper room, Christ told His disciples, "If you love Me, you will keep My commandments" (John 14:15). God's Word thunders in holy authority over His church.

Holy Sovereignty

In Revelation 1:16, John writes, "In His right hand He held seven stars." This is a picture of Christ's holy sovereignty. As Christ Himself explains in verse 20, the seven stars are the *angeloi* of the seven churches.

Commentators are divided regarding the identity of these seven stars. Some believe they refer to angels, but why would Christ send a message through John to angels back to the church? Furthermore, nowhere are angels ever given responsibility in church leadership in the New Testament. According to Hebrews 1:14, they are servants, not leaders.

It is best to see them as messengers. The word *angeloi* is

translated "messengers" in Luke 7:24 and 9:52, as well as in James 2:25. It's likely that they are messengers sent from the seven churches to visit John on Patmos, and that they will each return with the letter addressed to their congregation. Specifically, they could be pastoral representatives who came to receive the letters, each of them responsible to deliver God's Word to their churches. And the text says Christ held them in His right hand.

The point of John's vision is clear. What we see here is that the Lord has His pastors, His shepherds, secure in His sovereign care. As we see in the subsequent chapters of Revelation, most of the churches in Asia Minor were in bad shape. Certainly, some of those issues could have stemmed from poor leadership and conflicts within the churches. But here were seven men whom the Lord had in His hand.

Sometimes we can get discouraged about what goes on among pastors. We can get discouraged when pastors and church leaders don't teach and preach the Word and when they don't shepherd and lead the church. It's even more heartbreaking when lives of immorality and ungodliness are exposed, and an unfaithful pastor makes a shipwreck of his faith and a mockery of the gospel. Today we look at the confusion and disarray in the church, understanding that much of it is due to a lack of godly leadership. But at the same time, know this: the Lord always has His true shepherds in His hands. We can rest in the knowledge that there will always be, in every generation, those faithful shepherds whom He uses to edify and shepherd His church. The Lord will never leave His sheep without shepherds—true, faithful, and trustworthy shepherds. Even when it seems that dysfunction and disarray dominate the church, God always has His true shepherds in the palm of His sovereign care.

Holy Protection

Christians can be exposed to all manner of error, deceptions, aberrations, cults, and schisms. Spiritual dangers constantly arise from within the church and from the world outside. I worry about the threats that could strike the people whom God has entrusted to me. We must all do what we can to guard one another from spiritual peril. We have to watch and we have to warn. But we should also take comfort that we are not the church's last line of defense—Christ exercises holy protection over His church, as John saw vividly depicted in his vision: "Out of His mouth came a sharp two-edged sword" (Rev. 1:16).

What is this two-edged sword for? It's mentioned again in Revelation 2:12, where Jesus is identified again to the church at Pergamum as "the One who has the sharp two-edged sword." In that letter, Christ refers to the teaching of Balaam and the Nicolaitans and says, "I am coming to you quickly, and I will make war against them with the sword of My mouth" (v. 16). This is the sword that goes after the false teachers—the deceivers, fakes, frauds, hucksters, and con men who assault the church and bring in heresies. And we're reminded that the Lord is there with the sword to fight off the wolves and defend His own.

The true children of God—genuine believers in Christ— will not defect. They cannot be led astray or lost to apostasy.

First John 2:19 says, "They went out from us, but they were not really of us; for if they had been of us, they would have remained with us; but they went out, so that it would be shown that they all are not of us." In the end, no true believers will be eternally lost to that deception. God granted us the faith to repent and believe, and it's a permanent, unassailable gift. If we truly belong to Christ, we are bound to Him for eternity and secure under His protection.

Yet we still must watch over the church and guard God's people from spiritual threats. True believers cannot lose their salvation, but they can forfeit their joy and usefulness. They can sow confusion, doubt, and discouragement into their own lives. And they can cripple their spiritual growth by imbibing the lies of false teachers and charlatans. While God alone secures and protects our eternity with Him, He has called us to be on the lookout for one another (Acts 20:29–31).

Holy Testimony

Finally, we see one last facet of Christ's holiness in John's vision. In Revelation 1:16, we read, "His face was like the sun shining in its strength." Here is the glorious culmination of John's vision of the holy Christ moving in His church—His holy testimony. The whole face of the Son of Man is blazing like the sun. John is effectively saying, "His face shines like the sun in an unclouded sky at high noon." What John sees is the shekinah—the blazing, holy glory of God radiating from the face of Jesus Christ.

In the church and through the church, the Lord gives holy testimony. Paul writes in 2 Corinthians 4:6, "For God, who said, 'Light shall shine out of darkness,' is the One who has shone in our hearts to give the Light of the knowledge of the glory of God in the face of Christ." Do you know what Jesus is doing in His church? He's making the gospel believable by shining His glory through the godly character of His people. He's making the gospel attractive by displaying His glory through our transformed lives. As we let our light shine, men will see our good works and glorify our Father in heaven (Matt. 5:16). We are effectively the reflectors of the glory of God that shines in the face of Jesus Christ.

This is what John saw—at least, a vision of it. Everything that concerns us in the church concerns the Lord of the church far more. All that we would want the church to be—and all the Apostle John wanted the church to be—Jesus Christ is accomplishing as He moves in the midst of His people. He is empowering the church by His holy presence. He is interceding on behalf of believers. He is purging and purifying His church. He is teaching and commanding. He is sovereignly controlling its leadership. And He is using it as the instrument by which His shining glory illuminates a dark world.

Responding to Christ's Holiness

How should we respond to this vivid display of Christ's holiness? John's first reaction was fear. Revelation 1:17 says, "When I saw Him, I fell at His feet like a dead man." My friend R.C.

Sproul has become well known for understanding and artic-ulating "the trauma of the holiness of God," and that's what John is experiencing here. Why did John fall over like a dead man? For the same reason that Peter cried out in Luke 5:8, "Go away from me Lord, for I am a sinful man!" John was terrified to realize that he was in the presence of Holy God. If he could see the holy Christ, then the holy Christ could see him in all his wretchedness. He saw glory; Christ saw sin. And he was terrified—like Manoah, Job, Ezekiel, Isaiah, Daniel, Peter, and Paul. He was frightened into some kind of temporary trauma, but the experience quickly moved from fear to assurance.

Revelation 1:17 continues, "He placed His right hand on me." Was this a familiar touch to John? After all, we have to remember that John in particular loved to be close to Jesus. In his gospel, he called himself "the one who also had leaned back on [Jesus'] bosom" (John 21:20) rather than referring to him-self by name. He frequently referred to himself as "the disciple whom Jesus loved." He loved to be near Jesus, so I wonder if there was some familiarity in the Lord's reassuring touch. "He placed His right hand on me, saying, 'Do not be afraid; I am the first and the last, and the living One; and I was dead, and behold, I am alive forevermore, and I have the keys of death and of Hades'" (Rev. 1:17–18).

John did not need to worry. Jesus is eternal. He exists out-side of time, history, and creation. He is above and beyond us in every imaginable way. But He humbled Himself, took on the form of a man, and died and rose for us. The keys of death and hell don't hang on Satan's belt—he has no lasting power over us. Jesus alone holds those keys, and those who have embraced Him as Lord and Savior have nothing to fear.

In Revelation 1:19, Christ commands John to write the things he had seen, recording his vision, preserving it for the benefit of believers throughout all of church history. It's traumatizing to gaze at the glory and holiness of Christ—traumatizing, but crucial. We will never deal honestly with our sins until we have seen a vision of the holiness of God and Christ. And on this side of Christ's redeeming work, we live in the joyful assurance that the One who is so frightening is the same One who has paid the price for our sins in full, and whose holy justice has been satisfied. And amazingly, He still can use us to bring the light of His gospel to a world blinded by sin.

Revelation 1 gives us a rich glimpse of the Lord of the church, our holy Christ, and His ministry to His beloved redeemed church. We are His church, and He fellowships with us. It is for us that He unceasingly intercedes. It is us whom He purifies. It is us to whom He speaks through His Word with authority. It is us whom He protects. It is us who become the reflection of His glory. This is a mystery, that such unworthy souls could be called to such glorious privilege. May we always be stunned by this calling to represent the holy Christ, of whom we are not worthy, but in whom we shall eternally rejoice.

Chapter Three

JESUS IS
THE ONLY WAY

I have spent nearly half a century preaching messages and writing books to defend the true gospel message. During that time, that message has been consistently under attack, even from so-called evangelicals. When I was in seminary, we were equipped to defend the inerrancy of Scripture. We were prepared to defend the true ministry of the Holy Spirit, understand the proper paradigm of sanctification, and respond to the abuses of the charismatic movement. We learned how to battle liberalism, counter Catholicism, and deal with the cults, but the gospel seemed to be a settled issue in the evangelical world. Certainly, that is no longer the case.

Historically, the message of Christianity has always been the message of faith in Christ. The objective content of that message is found in Scripture. Since the New Testament era, true Christians have always believed that the only way sinners can be rescued from hell and be reconciled to God is through the gospel of Jesus Christ. For centuries, Christians have given their lives and shed their blood to make that message known. They have spent their fortunes to send missionaries to the farthest corners of the world. In many cases, those missionaries gave their lives to spread that exclusive and unique message. Throughout church history, the core message of Christianity has always been that salvation comes only to those who believe the truth about the person and work of Jesus Christ and receive it by faith alone.

So it is a pathetic irony that in our time, with greater means than ever to proclaim the glories of the gospel to the ends of the earth, the church has now become confused as to whether preaching the gospel is even necessary. Embarrassed by the realities of sin and hell, fearful of offending the perishing by calling them to repent and confess Jesus as Lord, and desperate to save God from being responsible for anyone's condemnation, we have raised questions about whether people even need to hear the gospel. After all, God loves you just the way you are, many will say.

We have questions about the lordship of Christ and the doctrine of justification. We have confusion about the doctrine of imputation and about the nature of faith and repentance. Many wonder openly, is it even necessary to believe in Jesus Christ? Others are confident it is not.

Apostles of Ambiguity

Today the word *evangelical* is so ambiguous that it doesn't really mean anything. Somewhere between 45 and 65 percent of so-called evangelical Christians are convinced that Jesus is not the only way to heaven. Not only that, there are some very popular and prominent evangelical leaders who are promoting that deviant theology. These apostles of ambiguity are happy to abandon biblical precision for the sake of a softer, more palatable pseudo-gospel of their own design.

During the 2008 presidential campaign, both candidates visited Rick Warren's Saddleback Church for back-to-back interviews. The event was the first of that election cycle to feature both candidates together, and it was broadcast on all the major news networks to a nationwide audience. In his interview with Senator John McCain of Arizona, the Republican candidate, Warren asked, "You've made no doubt about the fact that you are a Christian. You publically say you are a follower of Christ. What does that mean to you and how does faith work out in your life on a daily basis? What does it mean to you?" McCain responded, "It means I'm saved and forgiven," and went on to tell a story about his time as a prisoner of war. Warren simply replied, "That was just a gimme," as if to say, "That was so simple. You got it right. We don't need to discuss that any further."

But there was still much more that needed to be said. Saved *from what*? Forgiven *by whom*? McCain's answer lacked any specificity about the gospel at all. There was no mention of sin and no mention of Christ. There wasn't a word about the cross, the empty tomb, or the future glory that awaits. "Saved and forgiven" might have a hint of spirituality to it, but it leaves every vital gospel doctrine on the cutting room floor. Worst of all, Warren affirmed it as a sufficient answer.

A radically abridged and ambiguous view of the gospel has captivated the church today. We see the same thing whenever a prominent professing believer says his or her faith "is a very private thing." Let me suggest to you that if your faith is "a private thing," it's not the Christian faith. That personal, secret faith so many have concocted grants them no access to forgiveness and has no capacity to save. Jesus said, "Therefore everyone who confesses Me before men, I will also confess him before My Father who is in heaven" (Matt. 10:32). If you can't even muster the temerity to speak the name of Christ in public, what confidence can you have that He is faithfully interceding on your behalf? If you're ashamed of the gospel, it's a strong indication that you have yet to believe it. True, saving faith must not be hidden away. It ought to be the most public thing about you.

Renovating the Narrow Gate

Others are more overt in their obfuscation, intent on bulldozing heaven's narrow gate and creating an easier, wider point of ingress into God's eternal kingdom. Today there is a prominent and surging belief, often referred to as "natural theology," that suggests man inherently has the ability to reason himself to God—apart from any divine revelation or formal religion. Supposedly, man is able to discern enough about God from the natural world to satisfy any divine requirements for faith, without any insight from Scripture.

That theory is understandably popular in our pluralistic,

postmodern society, as it puts all the world's false religious systems on a seemingly equal footing with the Christian gospel. Moreover, it assaults the exclusivity of Christ, which is consistently and increasingly an intolerable notion to the world. And it was promoted by no less than Pope John Paul II.

In December 2000, before a crowd of more than thirty thousand people in St. Peter's Square, he said, "The gospel teaches us that those who live in accordance with the Beatitudes—the poor in spirit, the pure of heart, those who bear lovingly the sufferings of life—will enter God's kingdom."[1] We can concede that Catholics have already rejected the biblical teaching that salvation comes through faith in Jesus Christ alone. But flinging the doors of heaven open so wide renders even the Catholic system of works-salvation null and void. If heathens can be saved merely by living good and just lives, Rome's sacraments—along with the pontiff himself—are utterly useless.

Author Peter Kreeft (also a Roman Catholic) says in his book *Ecumenical Jihad* that Catholics, Christians, Buddhists, Muslims, and even atheists will be in heaven if they earnestly sought to find God. However, the biggest shock from *Ecumenical Jihad* is that evangelical leaders such as J.I. Packer and Charles Colson were happy to endorse Kreeft's nonsense.

Tragically, these divergent beliefs about salvation have successfully invaded the church. In a 1997 episode of his TV program *Hour of Power*, the televangelist Robert Schuller interviewed world-renowned Christian evangelist Billy Graham. Here is an excerpt from their conversation:

Graham: "I think everybody that loves Christ or knows Christ (whether they are conscious of it or not), they're members of the body of Christ. And I don't think we're going to see a great, sweeping revival that will turn the whole world to Christ at any time. . . . God's purpose for this age is to call out a people for His name. And that's what God is doing today. He's calling people out of the world for His name. Whether they come from the Muslim world, or the Buddhist world, or the Christian world, or the nonbelieving world. They are members of the body of Christ because they've been called by God. They may not even know the name of Jesus, but they know in their heart that they need something that they don't have, and they turn to the only light that they have, and I think they're saved and they're going to be with us in heaven."

Schuller: "What I hear you saying is that it's possible for Jesus Christ to come into human hearts and soul and life, even if they've been born in darkness and have never had exposure to the Bible. Is that a correct interpretation of what you're saying?"

Graham: "Yes it is, because I believe that. I've met people in various parts of the world in tribal situations, that they have never seen a Bible or heard about a Bible, and never heard of Jesus, but they've believed in their hearts that there was a god, and they've tried to live a life that was apart from the surrounding community in which they lived."

Schuller: "This is fantastic! I'm so thrilled to hear you say this. There's a wideness in God's mercy."

Graham: "There is. There definitely is."[2]

Regarding that supposed wideness in God's mercy, Clark Pinnock writes,

In our approach to other religions, we ought to begin with appreciation not with criticism. Only our traditions prevent it—not our theology. Let us heed Max Warren: "We remember that God has not left himself without witness in any nation at any time. When we approach the man of a faith other than our own, it will be in a spirit of expectancy to find out how God has been speaking to him and what new understandings of the grace and love of God we may ourselves discover in this encounter. Our first task in approaching another people, another culture, another religion, is to take off our shoes, for the place we are approaching is holy. Else we find ourselves treading on men's dreams. More seriously still, we may forget that God was here before our arrival."[3]

Pinnock sums up his view of Christ's exclusivity this way: "God the Logos has more going on by way of redemption than what happened in first century Palestine."[4]

That perspective also underlies Raimon Panikkar's book *The Unknown Christ of Hinduism*—a bizarre enough title in itself. In this book, Panikkar says the "good and bona fide Hindu as well as the good and bona fide Christian are saved by Christ—not by Hinduism or Christianity per se, but through their sacraments and, ultimately, through the *mysterion* active within the two religions."[5]

On and on it goes. There seems to be no end of pastors and evangelical leaders who believe the gospel of the New Testament is too narrow. Instead of faithfully preaching the truth of God's Word, they vainly attempt to identify a back door into heaven.

Such attempts openly contradict the clear teaching of Scripture. So here we are, forced to defend the exclusivity of Christ against constant assaults from *inside the church*. And the movement is not diminishing—if anything, it's quickly growing in this postmodern world, where tolerance dominates and everyone has a right to his own truth. In a culture that rejects absolute truth, Christians must be able to answer these attacks on the gospel.

Knowledge That Condemns

In Romans 1, Paul presents a strong case against the idea of natural theology. It is true that God reveals Himself in creation. He reveals Himself also in our consciences, through the moral law He's written on the human heart (Rom. 2:15). But that knowledge is not enough to save. Romans 1:18 says, "For the wrath of

God is revealed from heaven against all ungodliness and unrighteousness of men who suppress the truth in unrighteousness." The sinner, in his natural condition, is dead in trespasses and sins (Eph. 2:1), and dead means dead—he can't respond. He is lost, ignorant, and utterly blind to the glorious light of the gospel.

So even if the sinner, through nothing but his own powers of deduction, concludes that there is a powerful, law-giving God who has established the standard for morality, what can the sinner do with that truth? Does he innately have the capability to move from that to salvation? No, Paul tells us that the response of the unbelieving heart is to suppress the truth. He suppresses it in unrighteousness because he is, at his core, wicked, corrupt, sinful, and incapable of any true righteousness.

Paul continues in Romans 1:19–20: "Because that which is known about God is evident within them; for God made it evident to them. For since the creation of the world His invisible attributes, His eternal power and divine nature, have been clearly seen, being understood through what has been made." Why? So sinners can conjure their own salvation? No! Paul says, "so that they are without excuse" (v. 20). God's self-revelation through His creation is not enough to save sinners—it's only enough to damn them.

And "even though they knew God, they did not honor Him as God or give thanks, but they became futile in their speculations, and their foolish heart was darkened" (Rom. 1:21). Whatever faint glimmer of light a person might find on the path of reason and conscience quickly goes dark—actually, the sinner snuffs it out himself.

That truth is at the heart of the whole biblical understanding of salvation. This fact lies at the foundation of the gospel: the sinner is utterly unable and unwilling to believe the truth by himself. This might be the most important doctrine in all of Scripture, because if you get it wrong, you're going to be wrong about everything that follows.

People frequently get hung up on the sovereignty of God in salvation. But you can't hope to fathom God's work in salvation without first understanding the sinfulness of humanity. Only then is it clear that the only way a sinner can ever be saved is if God radically redeems and transforms him, giving life to the dead.

Apart from that intervening divine act, sinners' only instinct is to dishonor God. Spiritual darkness reigns in their hearts, and their thinking only becomes more futile and more bent against God. Paul says, "Professing to be wise, they became fools, and exchanged the glory of the incorruptible God for an image" (Rom. 1:22–23).

God's creation speaks to His character. He has planted testimony of Himself in the created world and woven it into the fabric of humanity. But the only thing sinful man can do is reject it, pervert it, and ignore it. The evidence of God's existence and nature may only amount to a faint, flickering flame in a world dominated by darkness, but sinners are all too eager to blow it out just the same. And for that reason, they stand justifiably condemned.

In the subsequent verses, Paul describes how the sinner's rejection of God leads to his utter degradation and corruption. It's a wicked and perverse descent—one we routinely see in the world around us. It's really the story of human history, repeated over and over in a futile, repulsive cycle of depraved destruction. In *The Intellectuals,* author Paul Johnson shares a series of stories about individuals including Rousseau, Kant, and other great thinkers who helped shape Western culture. What strikes you is not just their brilliance, but how perverse and deviant their lives were. Their intelligence is undeniable, but it couldn't save them from the disastrous degradation of Romans 1.

What does natural theology ultimately get us? Paul says it leads to "being filled with all unrighteousness, wickedness, greed, evil; full of envy, murder, strife, deceit, malice; they are gossips, slanderers, haters of God, insolent, arrogant, boastful, inventors of evil, disobedient to parents, without understanding, untrustworthy, unloving, unmerciful; and although they know the ordinance of God, that those who practice such things are worthy of death, they not only do the same, but also give hearty approval to those who practice them" (Rom. 1:29–32). Far from finding God on his own, the unrepentant man becomes a champion and a cheerleader for everything the Lord opposes.

The Foolish Cross

Unaided and unilluminated, in his natural condition and without the gospel, the sinner will never find a way to God. In fact, he won't be looking for it to begin with. "A natural man does not accept the things of the Spirit of God, for they are foolishness to him; and he cannot understand them, because they are spiritually appraised" (1 Cor. 2:14). He's spiritually dead and blind, with no hope of finding God on his own.

But even when sinners are presented with the gospel of the cross, they reject it. First Corinthians 1:18 says, "For the word of the cross is foolishness to those who are perishing." Even when a sinner has been shown the only way of salvation, he will ignore and dismiss it. On the other hand, 1 Corinthians 1:18 goes on to say, "But to us who are being saved it is the power of God." Man's supposed wisdom—the very thing that natural theology tells us will lead him to God—forces him to reject the message of the cross and the only power there is that can save him.

What does God think of man's wisdom? Paul continues in 1 Corinthians 1:19–20:

> For it is written,
>   "I will destroy the wisdom of the wise,
>   And the cleverness of the clever I will set aside."
>   Where is the wise man? Where is the scribe? Where is
> the debater of this age?

In other words, bring on the finest minds, the most articulate communicators, the best debaters—give me the elite, and I will show you a group of fools. In Acts 17, Paul is in Athens, and Scripture says, "His spirit was being provoked within him as he was observing the city full of idols" (Acts 17:16). In the Areopagus—the gathering place for all the philosophers and intellectuals of the day—he boldly confronted their laughable ignorance and proclaimed the only message by which they could be saved.

Men of Athens, I observe that you are very religious in all respects. For while I was passing through and examining the objects of your worship, I also found an altar with this inscription, "TO AN UNKNOWN GOD." Therefore what you worship in ignorance, this I proclaim to you. The God who made the world and all things in it, since He is Lord of heaven and earth, does not dwell in temples made with hands; nor is He served by human hands, as though He needed anything, since He Himself gives to all people life and breath and all things; . . . for in Him we live and move and exist, as even some of your own poets have said. . . . Therefore having overlooked the times of ignorance, God is now declaring to men that all people everywhere should repent, because He has fixed a day in which He will judge the world in righteousness through a Man whom He has appointed, having furnished proof to all men by raising Him from the dead. (Acts 17:22–31)

These were perhaps the finest minds in the world at the time, and the best they could do was put up a placard to serve as a safety net for any deities they had overlooked. That's maybe the best you can hope for from natural theology—the guilty sensation that you might have overlooked the true God of the universe.

Back to 1 Corinthians 1, and the pinnacle of the passage in verse 21: "For since in the wisdom of God the world through its wisdom did not come to know God, God was well-pleased through the foolishness of the message preached to save those who believe." That's effectively the Great Commission in different words. The only hope of salvation is through the preaching of the cross. Paul acknowledges that such a message is a stumbling block to Jews and pure stupidity to Gentiles (1 Cor. 1:23), and he's right. From a human perspective, believing that the horrific, humiliating death of a Jewish carpenter more than two thousand years ago has any impact on modern life—let alone offers any sort of substitutionary atonement for our sins—sounds like madness. But as Peter boldly exclaimed to the priests and leaders of Israel, "There is salvation in no one else; for there is no other name under heaven that has been given among men by which we must be saved" (Acts 4:12).

Why is that salvation found in Christ alone? Paul gives us the answer in 1 Corinthians 1:29–31: "So that no man may boast before God. But by His doing you are in Christ Jesus, who became to us wisdom from God, and righteousness and sanctification, and redemption, so that, just as it is written, 'Let him who boasts, boast in the Lord.'" Ultimately, the gospel is not for the proud, the arrogant, or those who believe they can get to God by themselves. God intentionally chose a foolish message to humble us and to guarantee that no one would boast in his or her own intelligence. He chose the cross to stifle any inclination in us to think we got to Him on our own. All the glory goes to God.

The Danger of Ignorant Zeal

We can't do justice to the exclusivity of the gospel of Christ without considering Romans 10. Regarding Israel, Paul writes in verse 1, "Brethren, my heart's desire and my prayer to God for them is for their salvation." This is vital to understand, because he's not talking about rank pagans here. Israel had the Old Testament. They believed in the God of Abraham, Isaac, and Jacob. They believed in the God who created the world and everything in it, who gave His law to Moses, who was the Redeemer and Savior of Israel. Prior to the writing of the New Testament, they were the sole possessors of God's written revelation. As God's chosen people, they had more spiritual light shed on them than anyone else in history. To them belonged "the adoption as sons, and the glory and the covenants and the giving of the Law and the temple service and the promises" (Rom. 9:4). But it wasn't enough. They were not saved.

Christ Himself continually pronounced judgment on apostate Israel. Even as He walked to the cross, while the professional mourning women were weeping over Him, He turned to them and said, "Stop weeping for Me, but weep for yourselves and for your children" (Luke 23:28). Jesus saw the whole nation of Israel as apostate. They had the Old Testament, but they had misrepresented its meaning and twisted its revelation into a system of salvation by works. As Paul explained, they had "a zeal for God, but not in accordance with knowledge" (Rom. 10:2). And religious zeal—no matter how vigorous and pious—is worthless if it's not grounded in God's truth.

Paul goes on to explain specifically why Israel's knowledge was lacking. "For not knowing about God's righteousness and seeking to establish their own, they did not subject themselves to the righteousness of God" (Rom. 10:3). In other words, Israel had underestimated God's righteousness and overestimated their ability to satisfy the righteous standard of His law. They completely misunderstood their own depravity and inability. Therefore, they failed to humble themselves like the publican in Luke 18:13, who pounded his breast in horror over his own wretchedness and said, "God be merciful to me, the sinner!"

Instead, the people of Israel were convinced of their own goodness and acceptability before God. They had a warped view of sin, a warped view of God's righteousness, and a warped view of their ability to attain salvation by their own efforts. Worse still, they had a severe misunderstanding of the cross of Christ. As Paul wrote in Romans 10:4, they didn't understand that "Christ is the end of the law for righteousness," that the only way we will ever be righteous is through the One who satisfied the law perfectly. Missing that pivotal point was a disaster for Israel's theology. It distorted their understanding of sin, Christ, and salvation. They sought to manufacture their own righteousness instead of relying on Christ's, which is available, as Paul says, "to everyone who believes" (Rom. 10:4). Their faith was firmly focused on their own works, not the completed work of Christ. Despite all the revelation God had given them—despite the incarnation of the Son of God Himself— they were not saved.

Israel's rejection of the Messiah was so wrenching to the

heart of Paul that in Romans 9, he says, "For I could wish that I myself were accursed, separated from Christ for the sake of my brethren, my kinsmen according to the flesh" (Rom. 9:3). He agonized personally over the apostasy of Israel.

But Paul's thoughts don't end in desperation. In Romans 10:13–14, he identifies the source of his hope: "'Whoever will call on the name of the Lord will be saved.' How then will they call on Him in whom they have not believed? How will they believe in Him whom they have not heard? And how will they hear without a preacher?"

Imagine for a moment that the theory of natural theology is correct—gospel preaching and evangelism are entirely unnecessary to see souls saved. That renders more than two thousand years of missionary work utterly futile. It means the incalculable sums that God's people have put into missions were a prodigious forfeiture and that the lives sacrificed for the sake of the gospel were a pathetic waste. The same goes for all the martyrs throughout church history—if it's true that people can get to heaven without knowing anything about Christ and with no exposure to the gospel, the martyrs were not heroes of our faith but fools who died worthless deaths for a nonexclusive gospel and in defense of meaningless biblical precision.

Make no mistake: the rise of postmodern Christianity and the supposed wideness in God's mercy isn't a harmless, potentially helpful theological perspective. It's a direct assault on the gospel work of the church and an affront to the integrity of countless believers who suffered and died throughout its history.

Paul knew better. He understood that he did not labor in vain, but that the gospel he preached, and that countless others after him preached, is the only hope in the world for those caught in the grip of self-righteousness. Romans 10:13–14 is his rallying cry to get busy about the work of the gospel. His case is clear: you can't be saved if you don't believe the gospel, and you can't believe the gospel if you haven't heard it.

Paul is so energized by the work of the gospel that he bursts into enthusiastic praise for God's faithful evangelists: "How beautiful are the feet of those who bring good news of good things!" (Rom. 10:15). He understood the farce of attempting to achieve your own salvation, and he was passionate about the only truth that could set sinners free.

In Romans 10:17, Paul continues, "So faith comes from hearing, and hearing by the word of Christ." That word of Christ was best summed up by the Lord Himself in John 14:6: "I am the way, and the truth, and the life; no one comes to the Father but through Me."

The world must hear the message of Jesus Christ, and we have the precious privilege of serving as His ambassadors and heralds. May we never be so content with our theology—never so satisfied with our salvation and sovereign grace—that we forget that our great God has not only saved us but has also called us to be the means by which He will save others. As long as He grants us breath, He has work for us to do. May we be faithful in the relentless proclamation of the glorious gospel of Christ, for His glory and the sake of His kingdom.

The Truth about Spiritual Warfare

Before we conclude this chapter, we need to think about spiritual warfare. Not the nonsense we see in the charismatic church, where a faith healer attempts to bind the demons of back pain and seasonal allergies through your television screen. True spiritual warfare isn't about parlor tricks or incantations. It's a tireless effort to which all believers have been called, an endless battle we must wage every day.

In his first epistle to the Corinthian church, Paul addressed a growing problem among the believers there. Not only was the church careless with their observance of the Lord's Table, but there were also many in the church who were still partaking in the idol feasts in the temples. Issuing a pastoral warning, Paul wrote, "What do I mean then? That a thing sacrificed to idols is anything, or that an idol is anything? No, but I say that the things which the Gentiles sacrifice, they sacrifice to demons and not to God" (1 Cor. 10:19–20). The point was simple: the idol itself might not represent a spiritual threat to believers, but the Corinthians should nonetheless respect the demonic realities behind such idolatry. Paul was making a comprehensive condemnation of all false religions. Worshiping anything other than the God of the Bible amounts to demon worship.

Such a conclusion is incompatible with the view of those who contend that somehow Hindus, Buddhists, and people of all other religions and worldviews can find their way to God through intuition, natural reason, and spiritual inclinations.

If Paul is correct (and he is), those other faiths don't present alternative avenues to heaven, nor does human reason present an alternate means of obtaining grace. The Apostle bluntly says that those pursuits can't lead people to God because they're actually demon worship. And while devotees of other religions wouldn't self-identify as demon worshipers, demons are nonetheless behind all false religion and at work in all false systems. Satan is the father of lies who masquerades as an angel of light, and his ministers disguise themselves as angels of light and bearers of the truth (2 Cor. 11:13–15).

We need to bring that understanding into Paul's second epistle to the Corinthians and the following exhortation: "For though we walk in the flesh, we do not war according to the flesh, for the weapons of our warfare are not of the flesh, but divinely powerful for the destruction of fortresses. We are destroying speculations and every lofty thing raised up against the knowledge of God, and we are taking every thought captive to the obedience of Christ" (2 Cor. 10:3–5). Paul is describing how the church must respond to false religion, worldly philosophies, psychologies, theories, and every other ideological fortress that stands in opposition to the truth of the gospel. Spiritual warfare is a battle against all anti-God ideas. He's calling believers to fight against the religions of demons.

The word Paul uses to describe these demonic lies is fascinating. The word translated as "fortress" is *ochurōma*; it speaks of a fortified stronghold. It could be a castle, a prison, or a tomb. All of those are fitting metaphors for false religions and faulty worldviews. Many people who pursue these alternative paths to God build their ideological fortress like a castle, but it quickly becomes a prison—and it ends up as their tomb, unless they're rescued and brought captive to Christ.

All of Satan's fortresses, regardless of how majestic and impressive they might appear, are damning prisons. All false religion is demonic, and people are not ascending to God through the means of demonic lies. No amount of good intentions, zealous piety, or reasoning capacity can claw anyone out of Satan's deceptive ideological tombs.

So when you encounter a person who devoutly follows some false religion, don't think that person is making the best effort he can to worship the true God. He is not merely on a more circuitous path to salvation. He is worshiping demons. God is not in those idols. Satan is in those idols, working to corrupt, distort, and confuse sinful man into believing he is pursuing truth. Paul says that's how we must perceive false religion, for the sake of those still caught in the clutches of Satan's lies.

In 2 Thessalonians 1, Paul gives us a powerful statement about God's judgment. Verses 7–9 speak of the return of Christ, "when the Lord Jesus will be revealed from heaven with His mighty angels in flaming fire, dealing out retribution to those who do not know God and to those who do not obey the gospel of our Lord Jesus. These will pay the penalty of eternal destruction." That's unmistakable. Paul leaves no room for a universalistic wideness in God's mercy. There is no back door to heaven. If you don't know the true God and believe in the Lord Jesus Christ, you will suffer the fury of God.

Natural theology cannot save anyone. All it can do is tie you to demonic lies and damn you—and it does so with stunning efficiency. It is perhaps the greatest grief of my heart that professing believers—those who claim to know and love the Lord—have severely impeded the church's missionary endeavor with this kind of heretical theology. At a time when God's people have the financial resources, the technology, and the means of transportation—when we have a global village that makes proclaiming the gospel easier than it's ever been—Satan has convinced many that the lost are fine the way they are. In fact, some have gone so far as to argue that we shouldn't take the gospel to the far reaches of the globe, since those who don't believe will be guilty of rejecting more of the truth. In the backward economy of natural theology, ignorance is preferable to illumination and preaching the gospel is dangerous rather than a means of deliverance.

We are appropriately grieved when God's name is dishonored and when false religions corrupt His truth and twist Scripture. We're right to grieve for the people who are ensnared by those lies and lost in their sin. But it is all the more grievous and gut-wrenching when people actively undermine the gospel and call it "Christianity." It brings such dishonor on God's name, and it proudly leads sinners further away from the truth.

May it be that we are faithful to the truth of Scripture and faithful to proclaim the gospel of Jesus Christ. And may God raise up a great force of people who, being faithful to that gospel, can be mightily used to bring that message of His glorious

Son—the only name through which salvation is available—to the ends of the earth. In spite of these demonic efforts, Christ will be exalted among the nations. May God give the church a heart to take the gospel to the ends of the earth, because men will perish without it. And may we be a part of that, starting where we are.

Chapter Four

JESUS IS
THE REDEEMER

Years ago, a mundane event turned into one of the more interesting and memorable moments of my life. I was flying from Los Angeles to El Paso, Texas, to speak at a men's conference. I was seated in the dreaded middle seat, slowly progressing toward my destination. The man in the window seat next to me was a Muslim from the Middle East. His presence was distinguished and palpable—he was in traditional dress and had a quiet demeanor. About thirty minutes into the flight, he looked over at me. I had my Bible out and was writing a few notes. He said, "Excuse me, sir. May I ask you a question?"

"Sure," I said, and he asked, "Is that a Bible?"

"Yes, it is a Bible."

"Oh," he replied, "Sir, can I ask you then another question?"

"Of course."

He said, "Can you tell me the difference between a Catholic, a Protestant, and a Baptist?"

That was not at all what I was expecting him to ask, but I was happy to oblige. And after I explained the difference between Catholics, Protestants, and Baptists, I said to him, "Now may I ask you a question?"

"Of course, of course," he said.

We were already talking about the nature of the gospel, but I wanted to bring the issue to his spiritual doorstep. I asked him, "Do Muslims sin?"

"Oh, yes. We have many, many sins."

Testing his self-awareness, I asked, "Well, do you commit them all the time?"

The honesty of his answer still stuns me. He said, "Yes. In fact, I am flying to El Paso to commit some sins."

"Really?" I said, somewhat surprised.

"Yes. I have just immigrated into the U.S. I came through the El Paso immigration center, and I met a girl there. We have arranged to meet this weekend to commit some sins."

Since he was clearly comfortable with blunt honesty, I said, "May I ask you another question? How does Allah feel about your sins?"

I had clearly found a sore spot. "Ah," he groaned, "it's very bad. I could go to hell forever."

"Really? Why don't you stop doing those sins?"

"I can't stop," he said.

I prodded a little further. "Do you have any hope that in spite of your sins, you might escape hell?"

I'll never forget what he said next. "I pray Allah will forgive me."

"Well, why would he do that?"

Somewhat hopelessly, he said, "I don't know. I just pray he will."

Here was the opportunity I had been pressing for. I said, "Well, let me tell you something. I know God personally, and I can promise you, He won't."

He looked at me like I was crazy, as if to say, *You know God personally, and you're in the middle seat on Southwest? You've got to be kidding me.* I was determined to push past his visible incredulity. "I know the one true God personally, and He cannot overlook your sin."

"But," I said, "I have some good news for you. There is forgiveness available. There is a way to be reconciled with God." And I went on to present the gospel to him. (I followed up with a letter in the weeks after, along with some biblical resources, but I never heard from him again.)

Messengers of Reconciliation

That's what I do—I tell people how to be reconciled to God. It's my job; it's my *life*. And it's yours, too, if you've been reconciled to God through Christ. That's what Christians do—it's our primary function. We preach the forgiveness of sins and redemption by God through the shed blood of Jesus Christ.

In 2 Corinthians 5:18–21, Paul speaks about the responsibility that we have as believers to proclaim the message of forgiveness—the message of reconciliation. And that's the pivotal word we need to understand as we consider this glorious text:

Now all these things are from God, who reconciled us to Himself through Christ and gave us the ministry of reconciliation, namely, that God was in Christ reconciling the world to Himself, not counting their trespasses against them, and He has committed to us the word of reconciliation.

Therefore, we are ambassadors for Christ, as though God were making an appeal through us; we beg you on behalf of Christ, be reconciled to God. He made Him who knew no sin to be sin on our behalf, so that we might become the righteousness of God in Him.

Five times in those verses, we see the word "reconcile" in some form, and the repetition is no mistake. The message of the gospel *is* the message of reconciliation. The alienated sinner can be reconciled to God. That's what we pray for, it's what we teach, and it's why we live. Some even die for it. It is the unparalleled message of reconciliation with God through the work of Christ. We have been given the ministry of reconciliation. In a sense, it's simply another way to describe the Great Commission—going into all the world, preaching the gospel to every creature, making disciples, baptizing, and teaching them to observe all the things that Christ has commanded (Matt. 28:18–20). The ministry of the gospel is the good news that sinners can be reconciled to God.

Left to himself, man cannot bring about such a reconciliation. To begin with, reconciliation has to be initiated by the offended party. David's tragic spiritual collapse included his affair with Bathsheba and the vicious murder of her husband, Uriah. But when he finally faced the totality of his wickedness, he understood his sin was ultimately an offense against God, first and foremost. In Psalm 51, he cries out in confession, "Against You, You only, I have sinned" (v. 4). Although we frequently sin against and offend one another, sin's primary characteristic is that in the end, it is an offense to God. And reconciliation for our lives of sin is available only if God, as the offended party, makes it possible.

From the human side, hell is inevitable. Damnation will occur. As hopeless sinners, we are dead—unable to awaken ourselves, shed our blindness, or bend the knee to God. There's nothing we can do to shift the affections of the heart away from sin and toward the Lord. As sinners, our destination is eternal punishment. As we've already seen, we have no powers within us, morally or spiritually, to devise a way of reconciliation. If there is ever going to be a change in the relationship, it has to come from God.

The good news—the greatest news—is that God has mercifully chosen to reconcile sinners to Himself. He has graciously made a way of redemption and restoration available to us through the sacrifice of His Son. Moreover, He has made those who are reconciled the agents of His redeeming work to a world in desperate need of it.

In 2 Corinthians 5:20, Paul calls us "ambassadors for Christ"—the Greek word is *presbeuomen* (related to *presbuteros*, a bishop or elder) and refers to representatives who bear responsibility. We are God's ambassadors, tasked with the solemn responsibility of bringing the word of reconciliation to sinners. And if we are going to effectively carry out this responsibility, we must understand the features of the message. What are the essentials that constitute the word of reconciliation?

One of my consistent disappointments in ministry is to see how few people who profess to know and love the Lord can give a detailed, coherent presentation of the gospel. It should not be difficult for Christians to explain and exalt the work of Christ in their lives. After all, it is the only reason we're still here. The only reason God has kept us in the world is for the work of evangelism. Yes, we're saved to worship, but God tolerates our imperfect worship on this side of eternity for the sake of adding to His kingdom. We're also saved to be sanctified, but God tolerates our inadequate, incomplete sanctification to keep us here to evangelize. He endures all our consistent errors and failures because He has work for us here that we cannot accomplish in heaven. And as we consider Paul's words in 2 Corinthians 5:18–21, we see four essential aspects of God's reconciling work and the glorious gospel we proclaim.

Reconciliation by the Will of God

First of all, we must understand that reconciliation is by the will of God. Paul begins our passage in 2 Corinthians 5:18 by saying, "Now all these things are from God." What things? We have to look back at what he was saying in verse 17. "Therefore if anyone is in Christ, he is a new creature; the old things passed away; behold, new things have come." All that is new in regeneration, all that accompanies the new birth, all that is transformed in conversion, and all that is made new again in salvation—all of it comes from God. His role in the reconciliation of man is a theme Paul returns to again and again in these verses: "God was in Christ reconciling the world to Himself" (v. 19). In verse 20, he describes the ministry of reconciliation "as though God were making an appeal through us." He doesn't want us to lose sight of the divine power behind this reconciling, redeeming work. No matter how He sees fit to use us, it's always God's work.

Throughout my ministry, I've tried to help people differentiate between the true gospel and the twisted, false gospel of the Roman Catholic Church. One of the many things that has corrupted that system so badly is its dependence on Mary. If Catholics want to make any progress from a spiritual standpoint, they instantly go to Mary. Why is that? Because she is perceived by most Catholics as more sympathetic, more compassionate, and more full of grace than any of the persons of the Trinity. So, the thinking goes, it's best to go first to Mary, because Jesus can't refuse His mother. If you can get Mary on your side, Jesus will always cave in to Mary, and then you're really on your way to God. That is why Mary dominates the Roman Catholic system—they believe she's the gateway to God's blessing and favor.

Not only is this a blasphemous lie, it's a direct assault on the nature and character of God. Far from being some distant, distracted deity, the God of Scripture is loving and compassionate. More than that, He is our Savior.

The notion that God is a loving and compassionate Savior

contradicts the core doctrines of the world's religions. If you study the history of religion, you'll be hard-pressed to find a savior god among them. When men and demons design gods, that's simply not how they design them. Demonic religious systems don't concoct deities anything like the God of the Bible. Instead, they generally range from indifferent to severely hostile. Just consider some of the false gods with whom the Israelites were enamored—starting with Baal.

The problem with Baal was that he didn't pay attention to people. To get his attention, the priests of Baal would leap around, screaming and slashing their skin with swords, as they did in their confrontation with Elijah (1 Kings 18:20–40). It reads like a horrific, stomach-churning display. And what did Elijah say about Baal? "Call out with a loud voice, for he is a god; either he is occupied or gone aside, or is on a journey, or perhaps he is asleep and needs to be awakened" (v. 27). That is a deity of demonic invention—a god of indifference who has to be awakened to the plight of his worshipers.

Worse still was the Canaanite god Molech. He was believed to be a scourge to mankind, and he could only be satiated with the sacrifice of infants and small children. His followers had to burn their babies to get his attention and fend off his wrath.

That's just a glimpse into the panoply of demonic false gods. And not one of them is a gracious, loving savior to his people.

The God of the Bible stands in sharp contrast. Consider the epistle of Titus. In it, Paul repeats over and over the short phrase "God our Savior." The pages of Scripture are loaded with references to God's gracious, saving nature—it's inescapable.

We need to understand that reconciliation does not start with the sinner, or some cosmic cry that God responds to. We don't have to ask God to accept the sinner—we don't have to coax Him into it through pressure or praise. He is not reluctant to save. Reconciliation begins with God—it's woven into His glorious nature. First Timothy 4:10 puts it as concisely as any verse in Scripture. Paul calls God "the Savior of all men, especially of believers."

In spite of the glorious truth it expresses, that verse can trip us up. Often people will ask, in what sense is God the Savior of all men? Critics and skeptics seize on that phrase in their attempts to spot contradictions between the Old and New Testaments. They ask, what kind of "Savior" God kills all those people? But that's not really the question. We don't sit in judgment of God's judgment. The question is not, why did God send bears out of the woods to destroy a group of boys who yelled "bald head" at a prophet (2 Kings 2:23–24)? The question is not, why did the ground open up and swallow people whole for violating Old Testament law (Num. 16)? The question is not, why did God displace and destroy the idolatrous Canaanites? The question is not, why did God destroy the globe and preserve only Noah and his family? Those questions are easy to answer: the wages of sin—no matter how great or small the sin might seem to us—is always death (Rom. 6:23).

The harder question to answer is this: Why are we still alive? Why has God allowed some sinners to live? Why does anyone survive the due penalty of their sin? The answer is that God, by nature, is a gracious and merciful Savior. He makes the rain to fall on the just and the unjust alike. He allows the unregenerate to fall in love and have families. He allows them to appreciate beautiful music, good food, laughter, and the other simple pleasures of life. They enjoy the blessings of His creation, when they rightly ought to be languishing in the torment of hell. God allows it because He is, by nature, a Savior. That's essentially what 1 Timothy 4 is saying. God is the Savior of all men in this sense: physically and temporally on a general level. If nothing else, we see the saving nature of God manifest in the fact that He grants sinners time to be reconciled to Him. Paul makes a similar point in Romans 2 when he says "the kindness of God leads you to repentance" (v. 4). Simply sparing unrepentant men and women from the due penalty of their sin—even temporarily—is an act of unfathomable kindness from God and evidence of His gracious, saving nature.

Luke 15:11–32 contains the greatest of Christ's parables—the story of the prodigal son—and it paints a vivid, humbling picture of God's saving nature. The hero of the parable is certainly not the Prodigal Son, nor is it his pharisaical brother. The hero is actually the father. And the most dramatic and instructive moment in the parable is when the father is looking off in the distance for any sign of his wretched, wandering son. The young man had shirked his duties and responsibilities to his father and family, cashed out his birthright, and departed for all the perverse pleasures of the gentile world. He had foolishly wasted his inheritance that rightly belonged to the family estate—funds that might have taken multiple generations to build up and secure. He had effectively stolen from his family to support his profligate lifestyle. And yet the father kept watch for any sign of his return.

And when he finally saw him, what did he do? He ran out to meet him. It's a stunning detail in the story—one that we can easily overlook with our twenty-first-century eyes. Put simply, Middle Eastern noblemen didn't run for anyone. We have literature from that time period that suggests that even among the Jews, it was considered a shame for a man to show his legs. It would have been unthinkable for a Middle Eastern nobleman to hike up his robes and run through the streets. But that's what this father did—actually, the Greek word indicates it was a full sprint. As fast as he could, with shameful abandon and no concern for propriety or his own dignity, this father sprinted out to meet his wayward son.

Don't forget that Jesus was telling this parable to Pharisees, among others. They would have been shocked to hear of the father running out to meet such a son. And when the father reached the young man, they likely expected the father to brutally slap him across the face to indicate his disdain for the son's wretched behavior. They might have expected the father to refuse to give the son a place in the house, or to make him sit covered in ashes in the middle of the village, heaping public shame and scorn on him for such an embarrassment. That's what the Pharisees would have expected, because it was the judgmental, holier-than-thou way they responded to sin.

But that's not what happened. Jesus said the father threw his arms around his son, kissed him all over his filthy head, put a ring on his finger, put a robe on him, and ushered him back into the household to celebrate his return. It's a vivid depiction of full reconciliation and full restoration to familial privileges.

The father is the Lord, who sprints after lost sinners, eager to rescue and redeem them from their wretched wickedness. He doesn't vengefully hold their sin over them, but gladly welcomes them into the joy of His eternal household. God and all of heaven rejoice over the repentance of one sinner, and the reconciliation of another prodigal. No one has to convince God to save the sinner—the work of reconciliation is born out of His nature as a Savior.

Reconciliation by the Act of Forgiveness

Paul highlights a second aspect of this work of reconciliation in 2 Corinthians 5:19. He writes, "God was in Christ reconciling the world to Himself, not counting their trespasses against them." True reconciliation requires God's forgiveness. The only way reconciliation can occur is if the offended party is willing to forgive and remove the barrier sin creates. The sinner cannot reconcile himself to God. Only the Lord can effect reconciliation by choosing not to count our trespasses against us.

That glorious promise reverberates throughout Scripture. Psalm 32:2 says, "How blessed is the man to whom the Lord does not impute iniquity." Paul echoes that sentiment in Romans 4:8 when he says, "Blessed is the man whose sin the Lord will not take into account." Micah 7:18 looked ahead to God's glorious forgiveness with these words: "Who is a God like You, who pardons iniquity and passes over the rebellious act of the remnant of His possession?" This is the message we bring to the world—that God, through Christ, can completely forgive their sins forever.

We might be tempted to think that apologetics is the great weapon of the church against the demonic philosophies and ideologies of the world. But sometimes—perhaps often—the work of the gospel is not an intellectual battle over truth and error. Ultimately, the most powerful thing we can say to a sinner is, "God will forgive all your sins forever, and welcome you into His presence." That is the good news. If people are not interested in that, intellectual arguments won't convince them. There has to be a sense of desperation and fear over their sin before they'll accept God's word of reconciliation. Under the guilt and anxiety of sin, there simply is no more powerful message that we can proclaim than the power of God to forgive sins.

Contrast that with the world's shoddy substitute for forgiveness. From person to person, forgiveness is more like a temporary truce than true reconciliation. It usually comes with an eye roll or through gritted teeth. Both sides agree to something like peace, but the offense is never truly forgiven or forgotten. We tend to carry around past wrongs like bullets— they're always chambered and ready to fire when there's the slightest hint of another offense. And we routinely hold that kind of ammunition against the ones we love the most.

It is not so with God. He will never call back some previous failure or a past sinful pattern. He's not keeping score. God doesn't just ignore our past offenses—He obliterates them. He forgives perfectly, completely, and eternally. That's what it means to be reconciled to Him—He has dealt with our sins once and for all. Through His gracious forgiveness, our sins are gone for good.

Reconciliation by the Response of Obedience

The means of our reconciliation to God—the sacrificial death of Christ, the perfect forgiveness God applies to our sin—are divine works. But there is a human component that goes along with it. We bear some responsibility, too, if we are to be reconciled and redeemed. Paul hints at it in 2 Corinthians 5:20: "We are ambassadors for Christ, as though God were making an appeal through us; we beg you on behalf of Christ, be reconciled to God."

In God's divine design, He has given each of us the responsibility to respond to the gospel in the obedience of faith. He doesn't pluck us out of this wicked world against our will—we're not robots that He merely has to reprogram. God is the initiator; He's the Savior. But it does not happen without a response.

The two little parables in Matthew 13 perfectly illustrate this point. Jesus said: "The kingdom of heaven is like a treasure hidden in the field, which a man found and hid again; and from joy over it he goes and sells all that he has and buys that field. Again, the kingdom of heaven is like a merchant seeking fine pearls, and upon finding one pearl of great value, he went and sold all that he had and bought it" (Matt. 13:44–46). Christ's point in those two parables is that if you want salvation, it will cost you everything.

Reconciliation to God isn't a little bump in the road of life—it's a radical transformation and reorientation of your entire being. We become new creatures entirely. Paul had just made that very point in 2 Corinthians 5:17: "If anyone is in Christ, he is a new creature; the old things passed away; behold, new things have come." Being reconciled to God means dying to our old selves, our old lives, and our old interests. Christ repeatedly urged His disciples to count the cost of following Him. It's why He told them, "If anyone wishes to come after Me, he must deny himself, and take up his cross and follow Me" (Matt. 16:24). Responding in obedience to God's call to be reconciled to Him can cost us everything—even our lives.

The rich young ruler understood that. It's why he walked away from Christ in shame (Luke 18:18–30). When Jesus told him to sell all his possessions and give everything to the poor, He wasn't offering the young man salvation by works. The money itself wasn't the point—it was a question of his willingness to do whatever the Lord told him to do. What would he give up for the sake of his eternal soul? It was a test of his obedience and what he valued most in his heart. And he failed miserably. Reconciliation to God doesn't happen on our terms, according to our schedules, when it's convenient for us. It's a radical redemption and transformation, and it requires us to be penitent, submissive, and completely sold out for God's purpose and work. Nothing less is acceptable. And because of that high cost, Paul says we have to "beg" sinners to be reconciled to God (2 Cor. 5:20).

When I was in college, I played football, and I had a coach who meant a lot to me personally. Throughout high school and college, he was the best coach I ever had. His name was Jim Brownfield, and he was a legend in southern California. He coached at every level of football. He was innovative, he was creative, and I cared about him a great deal.

I remember sitting next to him on the plane as we were flying up to San Francisco for a game. I took that opportunity to communicate the gospel to him with all my heart, but he rejected it. Through the years, I had opportunities to be with him here and there, at golf tournaments or other functions. He knew about my church and the ministry God has called me to, and he watched my life from a distance. And every time I was with him, I tried to talk to him about the Lord. He'd say, "I respect that. I respect you. But I'm not interested." I felt like I was always begging him, "Coach, this is the most important thing you'll ever do." But he was stubborn.

One day, I got a phone call. Coach was in the hospital. He had heart problems. Surgery hadn't helped, and it looked like he was about to die. When I arrived at the hospital, the nurse said to me, "He hasn't moved for three days. We haven't seen any motion, so I can't promise anything." I walked in the room, took his hand, and said, "Hey, Coach, it's Johnny Mac." He opened his eyes and smiled. I said, "Coach, one more time, can I beg you to be reconciled to God? Coach, you are the thief on the cross. You have no future. This has to be your time. Will you open your heart to Christ?" His head went up and down. He grabbed my hand, started to squeeze it, and reached his other arm over and grabbed my other hand. I was locked in his grip. The nurse came in and scolded me, saying, "Sir, you'll have to let go of him." I said, "I'm not holding on to him. He is holding on to me." With every last ounce of his strength, he was responding to the call of the gospel. For all those years, I had begged and pleaded with him—right down to the last hour. And as we prayed together in his hospital room, the Lord poured out his forgiveness and reconciled Coach Brownfield to Himself. I'm so glad I went to the hospital that day. I'm so thankful I had one more opportunity to beg him to be reconciled to God.

We ought to cling to the vital doctrine of God's sovereignty. But don't ever let your view of sovereignty overwhelm or obscure the fact that sinners have a responsibility to respond to God—and we have a responsibility to beg them to do so. God accomplishes His reconciling work through—not in spite of—the obedience of faith from those He calls to be reconciled.

Reconciliation by the Work of Substitution

All of that leads us to an unavoidable question: How can God be both just and the justifier of sinful men (cf. Rom. 3:26)? How can He reconcile sinners to Himself without compromising His righteousness and holiness?

Imagine you're a judge. Your job is to uphold and execute the law. It's the only standard you must adhere to, and you must do it unflinchingly. One day a man stands before you—a vile, wicked murderer. The evidence against him is ironclad. There's no doubt about his guilt—he openly admits it. He confesses what he did and says he's very sorry. Then he asks you to forgive him. And in spite of what the law says, in spite of your responsibility to dispatch justice, you grant him complete forgiveness and let him walk free. We'd certainly be horrified if human judges operated that way.

But that's exactly what our Judge has done. In spite of the clear standard of His law, and in spite of the overwhelming evidence of our sin and corruption, He sweeps aside our crimes, washes away our guilt, and sets us free from the due penalty of our sin. How can He do that and uphold His own holy law?

Paul gives us the glorious answer in 2 Corinthians 5:21—just fifteen Greek words that sum up the entire gospel and encapsulate God's ministry of reconciliation. Paul writes, "He made Him who knew no sin to be sin on our behalf, so that we might become the righteousness of God in Him." That is the doctrine of substitution, and that's how God can be both our just Judge and merciful justifier.

God "made Him who knew no sin"—which can only be a reference to Jesus Christ—"to be sin on our behalf." As we've already seen, Scripture testifies over and over to Christ's sinless perfection. The writer of Hebrews calls Him "holy, innocent, undefiled" (Heb. 7:26). Pontius Pilate—who had every incentive to find some flaw in the character and reputation of Jesus—said, "I find no guilt in Him" (John 19:6). The Father even spoke of the Son's implicit sinlessness, saying, "This is My beloved Son, in whom I am well-pleased" (Matt. 3:17). That same perfect, spotless, undefiled Son was "made . . . to be sin on our behalf" (2 Cor. 5:21).

Don't make the mistake, as some do, when it comes to understanding how God made Christ to "be sin." Many preachers in the Word of Faith movement, for example, teach that Paul is telling us that Jesus actually became a sinner on the cross. They say His sin forced Him to go to hell for three days, and that after He had suffered sufficiently, He was released through the resurrection. That is a blasphemous, ludicrous heresy. Ephesians 5 tells us Christ surrendered Himself without spot or blemish (vv. 25–27). On the cross He cried out, "My God, My God, why have You forsaken Me?" (Matt. 27:46). If He was a sinner, He would not have had to ask why He was punished.

So what is Paul saying when he tells us that God made Christ "to be sin on our behalf"? It means God treated Him as if He were a sinner. More than that, actually—God poured out on Him the full fury of His wrath against all the sins of all the people who would ever believe, as if Christ had committed them Himself. As a righteous Judge, He had no other choice. The just God of the universe had to punish sin justly—He had to pour out the full penalty on His Son to grant forgiveness to His elect people. And His justice demands that every sin that has ever been committed, by every person who has ever lived, will be punished—either in the eternal torment of hell or on Christ at the cross.

It's a humbling and profound thought that God treated Jesus on the cross as if He had lived my life and punished Him for every sin I have ever committed or ever will commit, to the full satisfaction of His justice. And for all who were included in the atonement—provided by the sacrifice of the Son by the glorious grace and mercy of God—the same is true.

All the judgment, all the torment, all the excruciating punishment was poured out on Christ as He died in our place. That's a breathtaking reality, especially when you consider that Jesus was only on the cross for about three hours. In that brief window of time, Christ paid for all the sins of all those whom God would one day reconcile to Himself. In the span of a scant few hours, He was "offered once to bear the sins of many" (Heb. 9:28). "He was pierced through for our transgressions, He was crushed for our iniquities; the chastening for our well-being fell upon Him, and by His scourging we are healed" (Isa. 53:5). First Peter 2:24 sums it up simply but powerfully: "He Himself bore our sins in His body on the cross, so that we might die to sin and live to righteousness." Through His suffering, Christ purchased our forgiveness. Through His sacrifice, He cleared the way for our reconciliation to God. He is our Redeemer King, our Lord and Lamb.

Amazingly, some people don't seem to think Christ's sacrifice was enough. They attempt to extend the atonement Christ purchased on the cross to the whole of humanity, as if He died for the whole human race. In so doing, they make His atoning sacrifice merely potentially effective. It must be actualized by the believing sinner. According to that notion, the price has already been paid for all humans—it's simply up to the sinner to cash it in. But a just God can't punish sin twice. He wouldn't lay the penalty for the sins of everyone on His Son only to later mete out that same punishment on those who didn't believe. A righteous Judge doesn't deliver double punishment. God did not punish His Son for our sins and then punish the unbelieving sinner for the same sins.

Furthermore, such a notion would mean that Jesus Christ did the same thing, in dying, for those in hell as He did for those in heaven. It would mean that He did not actually, really atone for anyone's sins. He just offered a potential atonement that is converted to a real one by the willing sinner. Christ died for no one in particular if He died for everyone. As Christ Himself explained, "I am the good shepherd; the good shepherd lays down His life for the sheep. . . . I am the good shepherd, and I know My own and My own know Me, even as the Father knows Me and I know the Father; and I lay down my life for the sheep" (John 10:11, 14–15). It's clear there was no limit to the punishment Christ could endure on the cross, but there would be no sense in enduring God's wrath if it didn't purchase redemption for those He would one day reconcile to Himself. Put simply, Christ is not the Redeemer for those who will not be redeemed.

There's more. Paul saves arguably the best news for last. Second Corinthians 5:21 concludes that God made Christ to be sin for us "so that we might become the righteousness of God in Him." Not only has God imputed our sins to Christ, He has imputed Christ's righteousness to us. God treated Jesus as a sinner, though He was not, so that He could treat us as if we were righteous, though we are not. In the most personal terms, God treated Christ on the cross as if He had lived my life, so He could treat me as if I had lived His life. That's the beautiful glory of the gospel. God sees us covered with the righteousness of His Son.

Many people—including some Bible scholars—wonder why Christ had to live through the humility of the incarnation for thirty-three years. Why didn't God just send Him down for a weekend—to be crucified on Friday and return to heaven on Sunday? Why wouldn't that suffice? Why did the Lord have to endure all the stages of life—most of them spent living in total obscurity?

The answer is the glorious truth we know as the doctrine of imputation. The writer of Hebrews says, "For we do not have a high priest who cannot sympathize with our weaknesses, but One who has been tempted in all things as we are, yet without sin" (Heb. 4:15). Christ had to live a complete life, fulfilling all righteousness, so it could one day be credited to us. The comprehensive nature of God's reconciliation is staggering. When God looked at the cross, He saw us; when He looks at us, He sees His Son. Our Lord did not just take on the punishment of our sins—He lived a holy, blameless life credited to us by faith. And we now stand before God fully reconciled to Him, cloaked in the righteousness of our blessed Redeemer.

Chapter Five

JESUS IS RIGHTEOUS

Before his conversion, Martin Luther was a fastidious but troubled monk. His conscience burned within him, and no amount of penance could ease or mitigate his guilt. In particular, the words of Romans 1:17 tormented his soul: "For in [the gospel] the righteousness of God is revealed from faith to faith." Describing that period of spiritual frustration, he wrote:

I greatly longed to understand Paul's Epistle to the Romans and nothing stood in the way but that one expression, "the justice of God," because I took it to mean that justice whereby God is just and deals justly in punishing the unjust. My situation was that, although an impeccable monk, I stood before God as a sinner troubled in conscience, and I had no confidence that my merit would assuage him. Therefore I did not love a just and angry God, but rather hated and murmured against him. Yet I clung to the dear Paul and had a great yearning to know what he meant.[1]

Luther could not understand God's justice without the critical truth we considered in the previous chapter—that God imputed our sins to Christ and imputes Christ's righteousness to us. We don't achieve salvation by living up to the perfect standard of God's law or manufacturing our own righteousness—as Luther discovered, that's impossible. Instead, we must rest in the righteousness God provides to us through faith. Paul sums it up in Philippians 3:9: "Not having a righteousness of my own derived from the Law, but that which is through faith in Christ, the righteousness which comes from God on the basis of faith."

The Holy Spirit eventually awakened Luther to that great truth. In the end, the Lord used the same verse that had once plagued his conscience to open his eyes to the grace of God. Luther was set free when he was finally able to understand the latter half of Romans 1:17: "For in [the gospel] the righteousness of God is revealed from faith to faith; as it is written, 'But the righteous man shall live by faith.'" Here's how he described his spiritual awakening:

> I saw the connection between the justice of God and the statement that "the just shall live by his faith." Then I grasped that the justice of God is that righteousness by which through grace and sheer mercy God justifies us through faith. Thereupon I felt myself to be reborn and to have gone through open doors into paradise.

The whole of Scripture took on a new meaning, and whereas before the "justice of God" had filled me with hate, now it became to me inexpressibly sweet in greater love. This passage of Paul became to me a gate to heaven.[2]

Luther understood the great and glorious truth of the gospel—that the righteousness God requires to accept a sinner is the very same righteousness He *provides* to that sinner through Jesus Christ. He saw that true justification can only come by faith. Paul sings the praises of that glorious truth throughout the early chapters of Romans. In Romans 3:21, he calls it the "righteousness of God" that is revealed "apart from the Law"; in Romans 3:22, it's "the righteousness of God through faith in Jesus Christ for all those who believe." Like Luther, Paul took great encouragement from the fact that "to the one who does not work, but believes in Him who justifies the ungodly, his faith is credited as righteousness" (Rom. 4:5).

We ought to be perpetually grateful for the righteousness of Christ and for a gracious, merciful God who applies it to us. We ought to be humbled and supremely thankful that when God looks at us, He sees His holy Son. Because on this side of eternity, our own righteousness is desperately lacking.

Dead to Sin

The resurrection of Lazarus gives us a graphic illustration of our predicament as regenerate Christians. Lazarus had been dead four days by the time the Lord arrived. Scripture tells us Christ purposely delayed His arrival in Bethany (John 11:6). Mary and Martha believed that if Jesus had shown up before Lazarus died, He would have been able to heal their brother (vv. 21, 32). However, it seems that they weren't convinced that He had the power to raise him from the dead. So Jesus waited long enough to display the full scope of His power.

Arriving at Lazarus' grave, He shockingly told the mourners to remove the stone. Stunned, Martha blurted out, "Lord, by this time he stinketh" (v. 39 KJV). The stench would have been severe, since the Jews did not embalm the dead. They dressed the body with perfumes and spices, but that didn't really mitigate the aroma of decaying flesh. It would have been very embarrassing to open the grave and have that awful smell spill out. Jesus, however, ignored her concern and cried with a loud voice, "Lazarus, come forth" (v. 43).

John records the miraculous event that followed: "The man who had died came forth, bound hand and foot with wrappings, and his face was wrapped around with a cloth" (v. 44). With his extremities bound, Lazarus likely shuffled out of his tomb looking much like a mummy. As Lazarus stood there, in full view of the stunned crowd, Christ uttered His famous words, "Unbind him, and let him go" (v. 44). As long as he remained wrapped in his stinking graveclothes, filled with the decay and stench of death, Lazarus was unable to fully express his new life.

In the same way, we have been raised from the dead through the power of Christ. Ours is a spiritual resurrection, not a physical one. But we are still bound in the rags of our previous existence. We have been raised, but we stink. That's the reality of our spiritual condition.

However, ours is actually a deeper and more persistent problem than the one Lazarus faced. His graveclothes were readily disposed of—he was wrapped in a linen shroud that just had to be unraveled. And once the shroud was removed, the stench of the corruption of death no longer clung to him. Our predicament cannot be resolved so quickly or so easily. Why? Because the remains of our former existence don't cling to us superficially like Lazarus' rags. We have a full-fledged dead carcass strapped to us. Paul calls it "the body of this death" in Romans 7:24. It's the lingering presence of sin that remains in our mortal flesh. We live anew in Christ, and yet the stench of death still courses through us. In Romans 8:23, Paul says believers "[wait] eagerly for . . . the redemption of our body." We long to be delivered from this body of death.

Justification and Sanctification

But weren't we already delivered in salvation? If we're still tethered to the rotting carcass of our flesh, what happened when we were saved?

The answer lies in the crucial difference between justification and sanctification. Both realities are rooted in the moment of salvation, but their nature is different. Justification is instantaneous, while sanctification is a process that will continue throughout the life of the believer. Justification is a formal decree from God that our guilt has been wiped away and we've been declared righteous in Christ. Sanctification is the process of actually growing in righteousness. It's the living out of the transformation that God has already worked in us.

Regarding that transforming work, Paul writes, "For if we have become united with Him in the likeness of His death, certainly we shall also be in the likeness of His resurrection, knowing this, that our old self was crucified with Him, in order that our body of sin might be done away with, so that we would no longer be slaves to sin" (Rom. 6:5–6). In simple terms, we're not who or what we used to be. Our old, sinful self is crucified and dead.

As a result, we are no longer slaves to sin, for those who have died are freed from sin. It no longer dominates our lives; it no longer has mastery over us. Its power is broken. As Paul says in Romans 6:11, "Consider yourselves to be dead to sin, but alive to God in Christ Jesus." We are like Lazarus: once we were dead, but now we are alive. Paul continues to stress the glorious news of our transformation: "For sin shall not be master over you" (Rom. 6:14). In Romans 6:17–18, he writes, "But thanks be to God that though you were slaves of sin, you became obedient from the heart to that form of teaching to which you were committed, and having been freed from sin, you became slaves of righteousness." And again in Romans 6:22: "But now having been freed from sin and enslaved to God, you derive your benefit, resulting in sanctification, and the outcome, eternal life."

In every sense, we are new creations in Christ. Salvation isn't merely addition. God's work of salvation is not simply stacking a new nature on top of our old nature. Our old selves have died, and through God's power, we are entirely new creatures. In fact, the transformation that takes place in salvation is more dramatic and radical than the change we will undergo when we pass from this life into eternity.

In the meantime, however, we are still bound to our sinful flesh. That's where the process of sanctification comes into play. Like justification, sanctification originates in the free grace of God. In fact, our sanctification begins simultaneously with our justification—in the moment God declares us righteous, He also begins to refine us through the process of sanctification. Both are also tied to the work of Christ—He is the source of our pardon and our purification. In sanctification, we break the sinful patterns of our former selves and grow in conformity to the likeness of Christ. The two realities are always linked—you can't be sanctified without being justified, and if you aren't being sanctified, there's no reason to believe you've truly been justified.

However, there are some distinct differences between justification and sanctification. In justification, the sinner is counted righteous because Christ's righteousness has been imputed to him. In sanctification, the sinner is actually being made righteous, though to a limited degree, through the work of the Spirit. Furthermore, our works play no part in justification, while they do play an important part in our sanctification. God commands us to "work out [our] salvation with fear and trembling" (Phil. 2:12). Finally, justification is an instantaneous and finished work—it doesn't grow, deepen, or improve in any way. On the other hand, sanctification is the progressive process by which God's people are always growing in godliness and spiritual maturity. It's an imperfect work, lasting for the rest of our lives, always incomplete until our glorification.

Is Perfection Possible?

That leads us to an important question: If we are dead to sin and free from its power, can we ever gain complete mastery over sin? That is, can we live sinless lives on this side of eternity? The short answer is no. But that doesn't stop many professing believers from preaching that sinless perfection *is* attainable in this life. The concept is often called "entire sanctification." Here is how it is explained in the articles of faith of the Church of the Nazarene:

> We believe that entire sanctification is that act of God, subsequent to regeneration, by which believers are made free from original sin or depravity, and brought into a state of entire devotement to God, and the holy obedience of love made perfect.
>
> It is wrought by the baptism with or infilling of the Holy Spirit, and comprehends in one experience the cleansing of the heart from sin and the abiding,

indwelling presence of the Holy Spirit, empowering the believer for life and service. Entire sanctification is provided by the blood of Jesus, is wrought instantaneously by grace through faith, preceded by entire consecration; and to this work and state of grace the Holy Spirit bears witness.

This experience is also known by various terms representing its different phases, such as "Christian perfection," "perfect love," "heart purity," "the baptism with or infilling of the Holy Spirit," "the fullness of the blessing," and "Christian holiness."

We believe that there is a marked distinction between a pure heart and mature character. The former is obtained in an instant, the result of entire sanctification; the latter is the result of growth in grace.[3]

That's a lot of words to say this: subsequent to salvation, one can instantaneously attain, by an act of free will through faith, sanctification that completely obliterates the reality of total depravity. This view denies that sanctification is a process of maturing; it asserts instead that sanctification is an instantaneous experience by faith that happens separately from spiritual maturity.

In his excellent work *Perfectionism*, the great Princeton theologian B.B. Warfield traces the influence of the doctrine of entire sanctification back to John Wesley. Perfectionism, as entire sanctification is also known, is an essential component of Wesleyan theology. Warfield goes on to show that the doctrine birthed the Holiness movement, which stresses the need for and goal of entire sanctification in believers' lives. The Holiness movement in turn has generated wave after wave of revivalistic campaigns and camp meetings that have crashed onto the shore of the church in various forms.

Though there are many differing tides, the one consistent fundamental is that perfectionist theology divides sanctification from justification. Specifically, justification and sanctification are considered to be two separate gifts of God. The idea is that sanctification is obtained in the same way as justification—by an act of faith, and in an instant rather than over a lifetime. It is not the same *act* as justification; it occurs at a later time, in a subsequent experience that is considered optional but highly desirable. Sanctification, in that sense, is the second work of grace.

In keeping with the Arminianism that undergirds them, perfectionist systems see both justification and sanctification as unstable. They can be lost. That makes sanctification a kind of self-fulfilling prophecy—you're only free from sin if you're free from sin. Your perfected godliness must be maintained. But even if it is lost, it may be recovered by another act of faith. So achieving entire sanctification could actually be a third or fourth work of grace, or the fiftieth. But when it happens, it is immediate and complete. Until it's not.

The only way to survive such consistent upheaval is to move the goalposts to a much more manageable distance. Put simply, proponents of this view redefine sin. For those who believe in perfectionism, in order for something to be a sin, it must be premeditated, intentional, and conscious. Nothing else qualifies. Unconscious and unintentional sins are referred to as "mistakes"; others corrupt the biblical language even further by calling them "temptations." As long as they're not sins, however, the illusion of perfection can stay in place.

You might be familiar with the name Oneida. Today it's a popular flatware company. But it is also a town in New York State, the history of which is far more complex and lurid. It was one of about fifty utopian communes founded in the wake of the ministry of the nineteenth-century revivalist Charles G. Finney. For thirty years, from 1849 to 1879, Oneida grew, until it included more than three hundred professing perfectionists. They followed the Arminianism of Finney and believed perfection was attainable in this life. They started many businesses to support the commune, including the flatware company that still operates today.

But in 1879, a shocking secret was uncovered: this community that professed to have achieved perfect love and perfect sanctification was all the while practicing communal marriage. Everyone was available to each other, and as soon as children reached puberty, they were inducted into this horrifying orgy. For decades, this and other abusive practices were carried on behind the closed doors of this self-proclaimed Christian perfectionist community—all of it excused by a woefully watered-down view of sin.

The same holds true in every variety of perfectionism: to make their theology work, advocates of perfectionism play fast and loose with biblical terminology. They are forced to redefine sin and holiness to accommodate reality.

Yet We Stinketh

Obviously, every perfectionist comes face-to-face with clear and abundant evidence that sin still resides in even the most devoted Christian. The perfectionists are not fooling us, and they're not really fooling themselves, either. When you have to redefine sin and holiness to get your life to meet an artificial standard, all you really end up with is a tortured conscience.

Scripture is unequivocal on the issue. Proverbs 20:9 asks rhetorically, "Who can say, 'I have cleansed my heart, I am pure from my sin'?" The obvious answer is: no one. First John 1:8 puts it bluntly: "If we say that we have no sin, we are deceiving ourselves and the truth is not in us." Verse 10 adds that claims to sinless perfection are an assault on the character of God and His Word: "If we say that we have not sinned, we make Him a liar and His word is not in us." In Galatians 5:17, Paul describes the war that rages within every believer: "For the flesh sets its desire against the Spirit, and the Spirit against the flesh; for these are in opposition to one another, so that you may not do the things that you please." If you have been justified by God and transformed into a new creature, you're well acquainted with the struggle he's describing.

Even Paul himself—a paragon of spiritual maturity and a hero to many believers—faced that internal spiritual battle. Near the end of his life, he wrote, "It is a trustworthy statement, deserving full acceptance, that Christ Jesus came into the world to save sinners, among whom I am foremost of all" (1 Tim. 1:15). He didn't say, "I *was* the chief of sinners"; he was referring to his present condition at the time. How can that be? Thomas Watson said, "Faith lives in a broken heart. . . . [It] always grows in a heart humbled for sin; in a weeping eye and a tearful conscience."[4] In other words, if you're being sanctified, you are increasingly aware of your sin. Far from the self-justifying claims of perfectionism, as believers grow in godliness, we also grow in the understanding of our own depravity and develop a growing hatred for the sin that still remains. As mature Christians, we understand better than ever the heights of Christ's holiness and we see more clearly than ever our own incapacity for righteousness.

Paul expressed the frustrations of that reality in Romans 7. In verse 14, he writes, "For we know that the Law is spiritual, but I am of flesh, sold into bondage to sin." That sounds like a contradiction of his earlier statements, that believers are dead to sin and freed from its oppressive rule. But Paul is not suggesting that he has been re-enslaved to sin. Instead, he's describing its lasting impact still at work in him. In verse 15, he continues, "For what I am doing, I do not understand; for I am not practicing what I would like to do, but I am doing the very thing I hate." He confesses the same dilemma again in verse 17: "So now, no longer am I the one doing it, but sin which dwells in me."

What Paul is describing here is the internal war he is waging—the same war all believers must wage—against the sin that still indwells him. Everything he said in the previous chapter of his epistle still stands—there is no true contradiction here. In the instant of his justification, Paul was created anew, given a new heart, and set free from the slavery of sin. But in his flesh, traces of his former existence still lingered. In Romans 7, Paul was wrestling with the graveclothes of his former life. What we hear in his words is the anguish that he is not yet completely free of the stench of death.

Paul understood as well as anyone the glorious realities of being crucified with Christ and the transformation that results. He was a radically different man than he had been before Christ, and throughout his epistles, he humbly celebrates the work God had accomplished in him. He was very careful to say that the new man created by God was holy and loved what is good, which is consistent with what he so clearly defined in Romans 6.

But Paul also understood that he would never be truly and completely free of his sinful self on this side of heaven: "For I know that nothing good dwells in me, that is, in my flesh; for the willing is present in me, but the doing of the good is not. For the good that I want, I do not do, but I practice the very evil that I do not want. But if I am doing the very thing I do not want, I am no longer the one doing it, but sin which dwells in me" (Rom. 7:18–20). Don't misunderstand this statement as Paul's attempt to shirk the responsibility for his sin. He was simply delineating between his will to please and glorify God and the sinful tendencies that were still present in his flesh. He longed to do the right thing, but he was persistently plagued by the flesh. This refers not just to the physical body; the flesh encompasses our humanness, what Paul called the "members"—our mind, will, emotions, and actions.

In these "members," Paul sensed the lingering stench of his former self. "I find then the principle that evil is present in me, the one who wants to do good. For I joyfully concur with the law of God in the inner man, but I see a different law in the members of my body, waging war against the law of my mind and making me a prisoner of the law of sin which is in my members" (Rom. 7:21–23). Paul saw his flesh like a prison, incarcerating him and tethering him to his former wickedness. It's why he cries out in Romans 7:24, "Wretched man that I am! Who will set me free from the body of this death?"

We ought to echo those cries. If we are in Christ, we are in the midst of the same battle Paul described. We're a holy seed trapped in an unholy shell. We're a redeemed new creation, caged in unredeemed flesh that affects our body, mind, emotions, will, affections, and actions.

Regarding Paul's cry for deliverance in Romans 7:24, Charles Spurgeon said:

> It was the custom of ancient tyrants, when they wished to put men to the most fearful punishments, to tie a dead body to them, placing the two back to back; and there was the living man, with a dead body closely strapped to him, rotting, putrid, corrupting, and this he must drag with him wherever he went. Now, this is just what the Christian has to do. He has within him the new life; he has a living and undying principle, which the Holy Spirit has put within him, but he feels that every day he has to drag about with him this dead

body, this body of death, a thing as loathsome, as hideous, as abominable to his new life, as a dead stinking carcase would be to a living man.[5]

That's the reality of our new life in Christ. We've been justified. We've been cloaked in His righteousness. But we still drag around the corpse of our former selves. So what are we to do about it?

Hacking Agag to Pieces

Mercifully, Paul doesn't end his discussion of the inner battle with sin in the desperation of Romans 7. In the next chapter, he writes, "So then, brethren, we are under obligation, not to the flesh, to live according to the flesh—for if you are living according to the flesh, you must die; but if by the Spirit you are putting to death the deeds of the body, you will live" (Rom. 8:12–13). The situation is not hopeless. While we will bear the stain and stench of our former lives, we do not have to surrender to them. Paul says believers fight the battle against their former selves. To use the language of the King James Bible, we must "mortify the flesh."

This is the distinctive behavior of true Christians—not imagining that they have no sin, but constantly endeavoring by the means of grace to mortify the sin that remains. Christians abstain from sin, keep themselves out of the way of temptation, and make no provision for the flesh. They are fixed on Christ, walking in the Spirit, meditating on Scripture, and praying fervently that they might not succumb to temptation. It is a lifelong battle that must be fought with passion daily.

The Old Testament provides us with a historical account that can act as an illustration of how we must deal with the sin in our lives. In 1 Samuel 15:1–2, Samuel says to Saul, "The LORD sent me to anoint you as king over His people, over Israel; now therefore, listen to the words of the LORD. Thus says the LORD of hosts, 'I will punish Amalek for what he did to Israel, how he set himself against him on the way while he was coming up from Egypt.'" This statement refers to a historical event found in Exodus 17:8–16 and recounted in Deuteronomy 25:17–19. Shortly after the exodus from Egypt, the Amalekites—who were descendants of Esau—staged a cowardly attack against the rear of Israel's massive convoy, slaughtering the weak and weary of Israel. The offense was so serious that God included in His law a promise to utterly blot out Amalek.

Now He was ready to pour out His wrath, and He ordered Saul, "Go and strike Amalek and utterly destroy all that he has, and do not spare him; but put to death both man and woman, child and infant, ox and sheep, camel and donkey" (1 Sam. 15:3). The Amalekites were vicious enemies of Israel, and God commanded Israel to obliterate them. The passage explains what happened next:

> So Saul defeated the Amalekites, from Havilah as you go to Shur, which is east of Egypt. He captured Agag the king of the Amalekites alive, and utterly destroyed all the people with the edge of the sword. But Saul and

the people spared Agag and the best of the sheep, the oxen, the fatlings, the lambs, and all that was good, and were not willing to destroy them utterly; but everything despised and worthless, that they utterly destroyed. (1 Sam. 15:7–9)

The Israelites did not obey God. They spared Agag and the best of the spoils from the victory. They took a dim view of God's justice and His wrath and decided they knew better. And their failure to obey would have dire consequences for Israel. First Samuel 15:23 records Samuel's words as he relayed God's prophetic condemnation: "For rebellion is as the sin of divination, and insubordination is as iniquity and idolatry. Because you have rejected the word of the LORD, He has also rejected you from being king." From that moment on, Saul's reign was effectively over. Failure to destroy the Amalekites cost Saul his throne and eliminated any hope of future kings from his line.

But God wasn't finished. The account continues: "Then Samuel said, 'Bring me Agag, the king of the Amalekites.' And Agag came to him cheerfully. And Agag said, 'Surely the bitterness of death is past.' But Samuel said, 'As your sword has made women childless, so shall your mother be childless among women.' And Samuel hewed Agag to pieces before the LORD at Gilgal" (1 Sam. 15:32–33). The vivid language paints a grisly picture, but this gruesome judgment was what the Lord had commanded.

Thanks to Saul's disobedience, the Amalekites would continue to plague Israel. Within a few short years, the reinvigorated tribe attacked the southern region of Israel, taking all the women and children captive (1 Sam. 30:1–5). David found and slaughtered them, but even then they weren't fully destroyed—Scripture tells us four hundred managed to escape (1 Sam. 30:16–17).

Five centuries later, in the book of Esther, a descendant of Agag shows up. His name was Haman, and he made another attempt to obliterate the Jews. Saul's failure to deal decisively with Agag led to centuries of trouble and struggle for Israel.

There is a lesson for us in the story of Agag: if we don't thoroughly and faithfully hack sin to pieces, it's coming back for us. And it will come back reinvigorated, sometimes stronger than ever. We must deal ruthlessly with the flesh that remains; we must hack vigorously at the graveclothes that still cling to us. We must, or it will revive and plunder our heart again. John Owen said, "Do you mortify; do you make it your daily work; be always at it whilst you live; cease not a day from this work; be killing sin or it will be killing you."[6] This is sanctification: a lifelong effort with a tremendous promise—"that He who began a good work in you will perfect it until the day of Christ Jesus" (Phil. 1:6).

What a wonderful thing it is to consider the reality of our spiritual struggle. Our consciences ought to resonate with this. We've been saved. We've been justified, regenerated, ransomed, and redeemed. We see evidence of new life pouring through us—a love for God's Word, for the fellowship of His people, for godliness and purity, and for the lost. All these are evidence of a transformed soul. But at the same time, we understand that we are still carrying the stench of the death that dominated us in our former lives, and we long for the day when we will be released from the body of this corruption. Until that time, may we kill sin with the mentality of Samuel, understanding that we can't allow the remaining sins to survive. We must take ruthless action against them continually. It's a task we cannot accomplish in our own strength—by God's grace, He strengthens us for the battle through His Spirit. May God grant us the grace to live righteously by faith.

Chapter Six

JESUS IS THE HEAD OF THE CHURCH

Jesus Christ is the Head of the church. But it's not enough simply to declare that Christ is the Head of the church. That biblical imagery was not chosen carelessly, and to fully appreciate its richness, we need to answer a few important questions.

What Is Headship?

First of all, what does *head* mean? Simply put, it means "ruling authority." However, feminists have tried to force us to redefine the word. For decades, they have worked to overthrow the clear biblical teaching on the roles of men and women in God's plan. In their efforts, these feminists have indirectly assaulted the Headship of Christ over His church, for, as we can see in Ephesians 5:23, Paul links the Headship of Christ to the headship of the husband: "The husband is the head of the wife, as Christ also is the head of the church." By attempting to redefine *head* and thereby to strip men of their authority in the home and the church, they in effect strip Christ of His authority.

One idea that critics propose is that *head* (Greek *kephalē*) in the New Testament means "source" and that it has no connotation of rule or authority. But in what sense is man the "source" of woman? Moreover, how is a husband the "source" of his wife? That interpretation is nonsense, and there is no linguistic support for it. Wayne Grudem has addressed this issue more thoroughly than anyone in the history of the church. In 1985, he studied the word *kephalē*. He examined 2,336 examples of its use in Greek literature. He went all the way from Homer in the eighth century BC to the church fathers in the fourth century AD. And in all instances when the word was used of a person and not a body part, it never had any other meaning than "governing, ruling authority."[1] That's what it means, and Scripture uses it in exactly that way—to say that Jesus is Head is to say that He is Lord.

Philippians 2:9–11 tells us, "For this reason also, God highly exalted Him, and bestowed on Him the name which is above every name, so that at the name of Jesus every knee will bow, of those who are in heaven and on earth and under the earth, and that every tongue will confess that Jesus Christ is Lord, to the glory of God the Father." When it says God gave Jesus "the name which is above every name," it's not referring to the name *Jesus*. The name above every name is clearly in verse 11: *Lord* (Greek *kurios*). To say *kephalē* is to say *kurios*. To say Christ is our Head is to say that we bow before Him. We bow as individuals, and the church bows to His sovereign rule.

In Matthew 28:18, Jesus says, "All authority has been given to Me." Headship means Christ is in charge; He is our governing authority and our sovereign Lord.

Who Gave Christ His Authority?

That leads us to another important question: Who made Christ the Head of the church? In Ephesians 1:17, Paul prays "that the God of our Lord Jesus Christ, the Father of glory, may give to you a spirit of wisdom and of revelation in the knowledge of Him." Paul is praying that God would help us have a comprehensive knowledge of Christ. He continues in verses 18–19, "I pray that the eyes of your heart may be enlightened, so that you will know what is the hope of His calling, what are the riches of the glory of His inheritance in the saints, and what is the surpassing greatness of His power toward us who believe." Paul is essentially praying through his own Christology as he prays for God to inform and perfect *our* Christology. In verses 19–20, he writes, "These are in accordance with the working of the strength of His might which He brought about in Christ, when He raised Him from the dead and seated Him at His right hand in the heavenly places." Paul is describing a majestic, exalted, transcendent Christ, "far above all rule and authority and power and dominion, and every name that is named, not only in this age but also in the one to come" (v. 21).

Consider this carefully: the sovereign God who chose us and called us, the sovereign God who gave us an eternal inheritance, the sovereign God who empowered and regenerated us for salvation, the sovereign God who sanctifies us and will one day glorify us—that God wants us to have a full understanding of the glory of Christ. God raised Him from the dead and seated Him in glory "far above." Paul is using extreme language here. Christ is not just above all other rulers and authorities— He is *infinitely* above. And "not only in this age but also in the one to come" (v. 21). Now and forever, Jesus is Lord.

Verses 22–23 continue: "And He put all things in subjection under His feet, and gave Him as head over all things to the church, which is His body." The language here is very specific: "He . . . gave Him as head over all things to the church." God gave the One who was already Head over the universe to the church, to be her Head. Colossians 1:18 says, "He is also head of the body, the church; and He is the beginning, the firstborn from the dead, so that He Himself will come to have first place in everything." God gave His beloved redeemed church the King of the universe to rule her.

Through Paul, the Holy Spirit uses this glorious language to express the love of God for His redeemed church. He didn't give us an angel such as Gabriel or Michael to be the head of the church. He didn't put us under the authority of one global pastor or prophet. Nor did He simply leave us under the care of gifted and faithful preachers, teachers, theologians, and evangelists—His undershepherds.

In His infinite wisdom and out of His boundless love, God gave us His Son, the Lord of the universe, to be our Head, our Bridegroom, and our Shepherd. And we are His body—as Colossians 2:19 says, Jesus is the head "from whom the entire

body, being supplied and held together by the joints and ligaments, grows with a growth which is from God." Christ reigns over us on the direct authority of the Father.

How Does Christ Rule?

If we understand that Christ is the Head of the church, and that the Father Himself gave Him that authority, only one question remains: How does Christ exercise His authority over His church? For the answer, we need to go back to Paul's letter to the Ephesians. Describing Christ's relationship to His church, Paul writes:

> For the husband is the head of the wife, as Christ also is the head of the church, He Himself being the Savior of the body. But as the church is subject to Christ, so also the wives ought to be to their husbands in everything.
>
> Husbands, love your wives, just as Christ also loved the church and gave Himself up for her, so that He might sanctify her, having cleansed her by the washing of water with the word, that He might present to Himself the church in all her glory, having no spot or wrinkle or any such thing; but that she would be holy and blameless. So husbands ought also to love their own wives as their own bodies. He who loves his own wife loves himself; for no one ever hated his own flesh, but nourishes and cherishes it, just as Christ also does the church, because we are members of His body. (Eph. 5:23–30)

Paul identifies several aspects to Christ's sovereign authority over His church. In verse 23, He is called "the Savior of the body"—He sacrificed Himself on her behalf. Verse 24 says He sovereignly supervises the church—"the church is subject" to Him. Verse 25 emphasizes again Christ's love for the church, reminding us that He "gave Himself up for her." Not only does He lovingly save the church, but verse 26 tells us that the Lord also sanctifies her, "having cleansed her by the washing of water with the word." Moreover, verse 27 tells us, He sovereignly secures His church: "that He might present to Himself the church in all her glory, having no spot or wrinkle or any such thing." In that day, she will be holy and blameless. And in the meantime, He sovereignly "nourishes and cherishes it" (v. 29), faithfully meeting all our needs.

It is no wonder, then, that Paul wrote to the Colossians, "See to it that no one takes you captive through philosophy and empty deception, according to the tradition of men, according to the elementary principles of the world, rather than according to Christ. For in Him all the fullness of Deity dwells in bodily form, and in Him you have been made complete, and He is the head over all rule and authority" (Col. 2:8–10). Paul couldn't bear to see any part of Christ's church forfeit the countless benefits of His gracious, loving Headship.

In his commentary on Colossians, John Calvin writes: "Hence, should anyone call us anywhere else than to Christ . . . he is empty and full of wind: let us, therefore, without concern, bid him farewell. . . . The constitution of the body [the church] will be in a right state, if simply the Head, which furnishes

the several members with everything that they have, is allowed, without any hindrance, to have the pre-eminence."[2]

God the Father loved His people so much that He gave us the supreme Bridegroom of the universe to be our Husband, to be our Lord, and to be our Head, in intimate leadership and direction. He fills us individually, and He fills us collectively as a church. We desire that Christ have preeminence, that He rule and reign supreme in His church.

Yet in spite of all that Scripture says, the battle has raged—inside the church—as Satan attempts to silence and obscure the Head of the church. In the scope of church history, the doctrine of Christ as the Head of the church has been a major point of contention—one that some have given their lives to defend. The true church has battled and bled to uphold this truth. It was, in fact, at the heart of the Reformation.

Laying the Reformation's Foundation

Jan Hus is well known to and beloved by many who are familiar with Reformation history. Hus, a forerunner to the Reformation, was born to peasants in Husinec, in what is now the Czech Republic. At age twenty, he shortened his name to Hus, which means "the goose." That nickname stuck—so much so that roughly one hundred years later, Martin Luther referred to Hus' vicious martyrdom as the "goose" being "cooked."

On July 6, 1415, Hus was dressed in his priestly robes and taken to the cathedral in Prague. There he was ushered before the public and brutally stripped of all those priestly garments.

He was tied to the stake, and tradition holds that "he was heard reciting the Psalms as the flames engulfed him."³ His executioners were so eager to rid the world of every bit of him that they actually disposed of his ashes in a lake. Those who revered him collected what little they could of his remains and returned them to Bohemia.

Hus' influence was not silenced by his execution. His books and sermons lived on in libraries across Europe, where they would eventually fall into the hands of a young monk named Martin Luther. Hus' commitment to Christ's authority resonated with Luther and helped ignite the powder keg of the Reformation. In fact, Luther looked to Hus as a hero.

Why was Jan Hus executed? If he was such a noble and beloved man, what led to his murder?

At an early age, Hus decided to become a priest. Since he had grown up in abject poverty, this was a good option for him, as it guaranteed a decent living. He was ordained in 1401 and became the preacher at Prague's Bethlehem Chapel, which seated three thousand people. He determined to preach in the language of the people and not in Latin, which set him apart from much of the rest of the Roman Catholic Church and made his teaching very attractive to the populace. He was also influenced by the writings of John Wycliffe, another forerunner of the Reformation. And when Hus preached, he actually taught the Scriptures, "desiring," as he put it, "to hold, believe, and assert whatever is contained in them as long as I have breath in me."⁴ In almost every way, Hus broke with the convention and practice of the Roman Catholic Church at that time.

Eventually, he was forbidden to preach and was excommunicated, but he refused to leave the pulpit. He just kept preaching at Bethlehem Chapel and grew more steadfast in his commitment to the authority of Scripture. The powers that be in the church, however, passed an edict that no citizen could receive communion or be buried on church grounds as long as Hus kept preaching. So, to spare the people, he stopped. In 1412, he retired to the countryside, where he taught and wrote feverishly.

His most important work was *De Ecclesia* (The church). It was read in public in Prague, and it contained several views that radically diverged from the teachings and traditions of the Roman Catholic Church. First, Hus explained that the church was made up of all the predestined believers of all ages. During the time of Wycliffe and Hus, the official position of the church was that the true church consisted only of the pope, the cardinals, the bishops, and the priests, and that laypeople were not real members. They only communed with the true church as they received the Eucharist, of which they were permitted to partake only of the bread.

In this same treatise on the church, Hus stated that the authority of the Bible is higher than the authority of the church. This was another radical idea in his day—one that he drew from Wycliffe and that would later heavily influence Luther's view of biblical authority.

He also taught that the reprehensible lives of some in church leadership made them unfit for positions of authority in ministry. He took a swipe at the whole corrupt system. Hus believed that Jesus is the Head of the church and that reprobate men were disqualified from any role in leadership whatsoever. He argued that the final authority over the church could not be a man who was subject to corruption "through ignorance or the love of money."[5] Instead, he explained, the church "always has had and now has Christ as its head, from whom it cannot fall away, for she is the bride knit to him, her head, by a love that never ends."[6] For these views, the Roman Catholic authorities burned him at the stake.

Opposing Rome's Ancient Lie

So, while the truth of Christ's Headship may seem to us somewhat innocuous, it is not so at all. In fact, the preservation of this truth has sailed down through the ages to us on a sea of blood. A century after Hus, the young Martin Luther engaged in the same fight. And his fight was for the honor of the true Head of the church. Luther said: "I am persuaded that if at this time, St. Peter, in person, should preach all the articles of Holy Scripture, and only deny the pope's authority, power, and primacy, and say, that the pope is not the head of all Christendom, that they would cause him to be hanged. Yea, if Christ himself were again on earth, and should preach, without all doubt the pope would crucify Him again."[7]

The Roman Catholic Church still holds to the lies of papal headship and papal infallibility. In defense of absolute papal authority, the First Vatican Council declared in no uncertain terms:

So, then, if anyone says that the Roman pontiff has merely an office of supervision and guidance, and not the full and supreme power of jurisdiction over the whole church, and this not only in matters of faith and morals, but also in those which concern the discipline and government of the church dispersed throughout the whole world; or that he has only the principal part, but not the absolute fullness, of this supreme power; or that this power of his is not ordinary and immediate both over all and each of the churches and over all and each of the pastors and faithful: let him be anathema.[8]

The Roman Catholic theologian Ludwig Ott explains the pope's supreme authority succinctly: "He himself is judged by nobody, because there is no higher judge on earth than he."[9]

Luther's response to papal authority helped set the course for the Reformation. He put it bluntly: "We here are of the conviction that the papacy is the seat of the true and real Antichrist, against whose deceit and vileness all is permitted for the salvation of souls. Personally I declare that I owe the Pope no other obedience than that to Antichrist."[10]

Describing the public reaction to Luther's assertions that the papacy fulfilled the biblical descriptions of the reign of Antichrist, the historian Jean-Henri Merle d'Aubigne wrote, "A holy terror seized upon their souls. It was Antichrist whom they beheld seated on the pontifical throne. This new idea, which derived greater strength from the prophetic descriptions launched forth by Luther into the midst of his contemporaries, inflicted the most terrible blow on Rome."[11]

Calvin concurred with Luther, writing in his *Institutes of the Christian Religion*: "To some we seem slanderers and railers when we call the Roman pontiff 'Antichrist.' But those who think so do not realize they are accusing Paul of intemperate language, after whom we speak, indeed, so speak from his very lips. And lest anyone object that we wickedly twist Paul's words (which apply to another) against the Roman pontiff, I shall briefly show that these cannot be understood otherwise than of the papacy."[12]

Recounting the history of the Reformation in Scotland, John Knox declared unequivocally, "The Pope is the head of the Kirk of Antichrist."[13] The Westminster Confession of Faith came to the same conclusion: "There is no other head of the Church but the Lord Jesus Christ, Nor can the Pope of Rome, in any sense, be head thereof; but is that Antichrist, that man of sin, and son of perdition, that exalts himself, in the Church against Christ and all that is called God."[14]

These examples should make clear that there has been a long and fierce battle to uphold the Headship of Christ over His church. Throughout church history, God's people have had to assert and defend His leadership over His church. They've had to step out from under the folds of reprobate robed popes and a vile, illegitimate priesthood and cling to the authority and Headship of the Lord Jesus Christ. Opposing Rome's lies was a sure path to excommunication and persecution—and it often led to death as well.

The Scottish Covenanters

Of particular interest to me is the Scottish chapter in this age-old story. In the seventeenth century, the war over the headship of the church came to Scotland. By then, it wasn't just a question of choosing between Jesus Christ and the pope—others were vying for their own authority over the church as well. Remember that the Church of England was founded out of King Henry VIII's desire to divorce and remarry and the pope's unwillingness to grant him that right. While Anglicanism represented a reformation from some of Rome's errors, it also foolishly repeated others—including the declaration that the ruling monarch would serve as the supreme head of the Church of England. That was simply a papacy by another name. In the tumultuous years that followed, England's religious loyalties lurched back and forth between Roman Catholicism and Anglicanism.

When Charles I came to power, he was determined to reassert Anglican authority over the Scottish church, which rebelled against the notion of any human headship for the church. Together with William Laud, archbishop of Canterbury, Charles I concocted a new liturgical book to be imposed upon the Scottish church by the Crown. In his book *The Preachers of Scotland*, written in 1888, William Blaikie writes, "The attempt by the State party to force a new liturgy on the Church, the use of which should be binding under the highest penalties, showed a determination to set aside Christ's authority, and tyrannise over His heritage even in the most sacred region of worship."[15]

You may have heard of the famous incident at St. Giles Cathedral on the Royal Mile in Edinburgh that involved a young lady named Jenny Geddes. She was in attendance for a Lord's Day service on July 23, 1637. When the dean of Edinburgh, James Hannay, introduced the new book of liturgy, tradition holds that Geddes stood up in protest, picked up her prayer stool, and threw it at Hannay's head, castigating him for daring to say the Mass. Her outburst launched a riot and birthed a conflict that continued for decades.

A group of Scots who were opposed to the Anglican liturgy composed and presented a document called the National Covenant in 1638. It affirmed support for the historic Reformed faith and was signed by thousands, signifying their allegiance to Christ over the king. Blaikie writes, "By the force of reaction the Church was thrown upon the more full assertion of Christ's claims as Head of the Church, and the glorious privilege of the Church to follow her divine Head."[16]

Beginning with the signing of the National Covenant, the Scots endured a decade of tumult and war, during which the church refined its theology in the forge of persecution. The Headship of Christ was the anchor for the Covenanters' faith. "The more this truth was thought of, the more glorious did it seem," Blaikie writes.[17] So many times in the history of the church, that's what happens: when people fight to preserve and protect the truth of Scripture, they find a richness to the Word of God they never would have discovered had there been no battle. Blaikie goes on:

Every vision of the Apocalypse acquired new interest when it was remembered that the true Head of the Reformed Church of Scotland was no other than the glorious King exalted to such honour there, the Lamb in the midst of the throne, having on His head many crowns, and surrounded by elders and living creatures, and thousands of thousands crying with a loud voice, Worthy is the Lamb that was slain! The men of those times did not, like so many now, deem it enough to recognize Christ's headship over themselves personally; they joined to that, with all the ardor of their nature, His headship over the whole Church. To repudiate the one was as great a crime and as great a folly as to repudiate the other. To deny Him His place as King in Zion was to imperil their personal relation to Him almost as much as to deny His atonement or His mediation.[18]

Across Scotland, a terrible slaughter took place as the English tried to suppress the ferment of the Covenanters. I've been to the area in Edinburgh where the massacres took place. I've seen the places around St. Giles where they displayed the severed heads of the Covenanters who confessed Christ as the Head of the church. But as gruesome as the persecution was, the faithful resolve of the Covenanters stands as a powerful example to us.

There's a wonderful story about a seventeen-year-old girl who affirmed that Christ is the Head of the church. They took her out to the Firth of Forth, where the River Forth flows into the North Sea, and propped her up on a stake at low tide. As the tide rolled back in, her executioners stood on the shore and badgered her to recant before she drowned. Next to her they had positioned an older woman, and these dear ladies drowned together for the sake of their Savior. Many others were drowned, hanged, beheaded, chopped up, and tortured to death through every cruel means imaginable. The persecution was merciless— even children were tortured. All of them willingly went to their graves defending Christ's authority over His church.

The Battle Continues

The violence in Scotland eventually subsided, but the battle over Christ's authority in the church has continued unabated. Centuries later, in a sermon titled "The Head of the Church," Charles Spurgeon said:

> Of all the dreams that ever deluded men, and probably of all blasphemies that ever were uttered, there has never been one which is more absurd and which is more fruitful in all manner of mischief than the idea that the Bishop of Rome can be the head of the church of Jesus Christ. No; these popes die, and are not; and how could the church live if its head were dead? The true Head ever liveth, and the church ever liveth in him.[19]

In another sermon titled "Christ Glorified," Spurgeon further explained:

Christ did not redeem his Church with his blood that the Pope might come in and steal away the glory. He never came from heaven to earth, and poured out his very heart that he might purchase his people that a poor sinner, a mere man, should be set upon high to be admired by all the nations, and to call himself God's representative on earth. Christ has always been the head of his church.[20]

Spurgeon clearly loved and cherished the doctrine of Christ's Headship over the church. In his sermon "Jesus, Our Lord," he described the rank blasphemy of usurping that role:

The Church of God, in a very special manner, calls Jesus "our Lord," for there is not, and there cannot be any head of the Church except the Lord Jesus Christ. It is awful blasphemy for any man on earth to call himself Christ's vicar and the head of the church, and it is a usurpation of the crown rights of King Jesus for any king or queen to be called the head of the church, for the true Church of Jesus Christ can have no head but Jesus Christ himself. I am thankful that there is no head to the church of which I am a member save Jesus Christ himself, nor dare I be a member of any church which would consent to any headship but his.[21]

Jonathan Edwards spoke to this issue as well:

Christians are one society, one body politic. . . . They are subject to the same King, Jesus Christ. He is the head of the church, he is the head of this body politic. Indeed all men are subject to the power and providence of this King; but those who are in his kingdom of grace, all acknowledge the same King, own his rightful sovereignty over them, are willing to be subject to him, to submit to his will, and yield obedience to his commands.[22]

Virtually every era of church history has had to defend the authority of Christ. Today, for example, modern liberal theologians deny Christ's Headship by saying that Jesus is dead. If you don't believe in the resurrection, He's certainly not the Head of the church. He's just a dead martyr. By denying His resurrection, they also deny His deity and His authority. It's a chain reaction of bad theology that, in the end, allows them to dismiss the Word of God as uninspired and the Son of God as a martyred rabbi.

Similarly, the seeker-sensitive movement strips Christ of His Headship. Adherents of this movement silence His rule by removing His Word from its rightful place of authority, instead letting the whims and wants of the world dictate how the church operates. The sideshow inevitably becomes the main event and the preaching of the gospel is pushed further and further to the periphery. In the end, they might attract a crowd, but they've got nothing of spiritual substance to offer the lost once they show up.

The emerging church movement was essentially one big swipe at the Lord's leadership over His church. Its leaders denied Christ's authority and attempted to sit in judgment of God's Word, preaching uncertainty in place of the clarity of Scripture. Emphasizing what they called "the hermeneutics of humility," they viewed certainty as proud, intolerant, and divisive.

In a blog post titled "Certitude Can Be Idolatrous," John Armstrong—one of the movement's vocal proponents—compared Christians who "have a high level of certitude" to dictators and tyrants.[23] Describing his own battle against certainty, he said, "I have been forced, upon deeper reflection about theological method, to give up what I call epistemological certitude. . . . If there is a foundation in Christian theology, and I believe that there must be, then it is not found in the Church, Scripture, tradition, or culture. . . . Theology must be a humble human attempt to 'hear [God]'—never about rational approaches to texts."[24]

In his book *Generous Orthodoxy*, Brian McLaren famously declared, "I have gone out of my way to be provocative, mischievous, and unclear, reflecting my belief that clarity is sometimes overrated, and that shock, obscurity, playfulness, and intrigue (carefully articulated) often stimulate more thought than clarity."[25] The love of confusion, debate, and academic uncertainty quickly ran the movement aground.

We are stunned at those absurd claims. How can the Lord speak to His church if we don't know what He means by what He says? How can He speak to His church if He's dead?

How can He speak to His church if the Bible is taken out and replaced with sideshow entertainment?

Rome said the Bible is unclear—that it's beyond the comprehension of the common man. Roman Catholic dogma claims the only way anyone can understand Scripture is if the infallible church interprets it. Roman Catholicism fought to keep the Bible out of the language of the people, and it killed William Tyndale for giving people copies of Scripture. To this day, it's the pope and his bishops who determine what God's Word says and what it means. Rome's vicious doctrinal stranglehold on hundreds of millions around the globe proves you can strip the Lord of the church of His authority in many ways—not just with bloodshed.

When you consider the state of twenty-first-century society and its aggressive opposition to authority in any form, it's clear that the fight for the Headship of Christ will only intensify. You need only look at the current trends in evangelicalism for proof.

Today, many believers perpetually float between churches, going wherever their tastes and preferences lead them, without being planted in a Bible-preaching, doctrinally sound congregation where Scripture is the authority. It is massively popular to bring a spirit of entrepreneurialism to the church, emphasizing creativity, novelty, ingenuity, and cleverness over biblical authority and doctrine. And too many have no tolerance for propositional truth, expository preaching, or godly shepherds—they want entertaining, motivational speeches delivered by bad-boy, rock-star pulpiteers. Such tendencies, tastes, and interests do not reflect a heart that is bowing low to

the authority of Christ—they reflect the rebellious self-interest of the world.

Nonbiblical ministry, non-expository preaching, and non-doctrinal teaching usurp Christ's Headship, silencing His voice to His church. They give honor to proud independence and autonomy as if such traits were virtues. These approaches strip the church of the mind of Christ, build indifference and ignorance toward Scripture, remove protection from error and sin, eliminate transcendence and clarity, cripple worship, produce compromisers, and cheat God's people of the glory of their Lord in all His fullness.

Throughout church history, the truth of Christ's Headship has been under assault. Inasmuch as we're able, we must carry on the fight to defend Christ's authority over His church, which He bought with His blood.

NOTES

Chapter One

1 Quoted from the Church of Scientology's OT VIII training materials, entered into the public record as part of a federal court case called *Church of Scientology International v. Fishman and Geertz*. The church disputes the material as a forgery.

Chapter Three

1 "Pope Takes Inclusive View of Salvation," *Los Angeles Times*, Religion News Service, December 9, 2000.

2 *Hour of Power*, March 31, 1997.

3 Clark Pinnock, *A Wideness in God's Mercy* (Grand Rapids, Mich.: Zondervan, 1992), 141.

4 Ibid., 77.

5 Raimon Panikkar, *The Unknown Christ of Hinduism* (Maryknoll, N.Y.: Orbis, 1981), 54.

Chapter Five

1 Cited in Roland Bainton, *Here I Stand* (New York: Abingdon, 1950), 65.

2 Ibid.

3 "Articles of Faith," Church of the Nazarene, accessed June 9, 2017, http://www.nazarene.org/articles-faith.

4 Thomas Watson, *A Body of Divinity* (Grand Rapids, Mich.: Sovereign Grace, n.d.), 369.

5 Charles Haddon Spurgeon, "The Fainting Warrior," Sermon 235 in *The New Park Street Pulpit*, vol. 5 (London: Passmore & Alabaster, 1859), 83.

6 John Owen, *The Works of John Owen*, vol. 6 (1853; repr. Edinburgh, Scotland: Banner of Truth, 1967), 9.

NOTES

Chapter Six

1 Wayne Grudem, "Does Κεφαλη ("Head") Mean "Source" or "Authority Over" in Greek Literature? A Survey of 2,336 Examples," *Trinity Journal* no. 6.1 (Spring 1985): 38–59.

2 *Calvin's Commentaries*, vol. 21 (Grand Rapids, Mich.: Baker, 2003), 198.

3 Mark Galli and Ted Olson eds., *131 Christians Everyone Should Know* (Nashville, Tenn.: Broadman & Holman, 2000), 371.

4 Ibid., 370.

5 Ibid., 371.

6 John Huss, *De Ecclesia*, trans. David S. Schaff (New York: Scribner's Sons, 1915), 29.

7 Martin Luther, *The Table Talk of Martin Luther*, ed. and trans. William Hazlitt (London: David Bogue, 1848), 234.

8 First Vatican Council, "*Pastor aeturnus*: Dogmatic Constitution of the Church," July 18, 1870, 3.9.

9 Ludwig Ott, *Fundamentals of Catholic Dogma* (St. Louis: B. Herder, 1964), 286.

10 Le Roy Edwin Froom, *The Prophetic Faith of Our Fathers*, vol. 2 (Washington, D.C.: Review and Herald, 1948), 256.

11 Jean-Henri Merle d'Aubigne, *History of the Reformation of the Sixteenth Century* (Grand Rapids, Mich.: Baker, 1976), 215.

12 John Calvin, *Institutes of the Christian Religion*, ed. John T. McNeill, trans. Ford Lewis Battles (Philadelphia: Westminster, 1960), 4.7.25.

13 John Knox, *The History of the Reformation of Religion in Scotland* (London: Andrew Melrose, 1905), 3.

14 Westminster Confession of Faith (1647) 25.6.

15 William Blaikie, *The Preachers of Scotland* (Edinburgh, Scotland: Banner of Truth, 2001), 97.

16 Ibid.

17 Ibid.

18 Ibid., 97–98.

19 Charles Haddon Spurgeon, "The Head of the Church," Sermon 839 in *The Metropolitan Tabernacle Pulpit*, vol. 14 (London: Passmore & Alabaster, 1868), 621.

20 Charles Haddon Spurgeon, "Christ Glorified," Sermon 3436 in *The Metropolitan Tabernacle Pulpit*, vol. 60 (London: Passmore & Alabaster, 1914), 592.

21 Charles Haddon Spurgeon, "Jesus, Our Lord," Sermon 2806 in *The Metropolitan Tabernacle Pulpit*, vol. 48 (London: Passmore & Alabaster, 1902), 558.

22 Jonathan Edwards, "Christians: A Chosen Generation, A Royal Priesthood, An Holy Nation, And a Peculiar People," *The Works of Jonathan Edwards*, vol. 2 (Edinburgh, Scotland: Banner of Truth, 1974), 945.

23 John Armstrong, "Certitude Can Be Idolatrous," June 30, 2005, http://johnharmstrong.com.

24 John Armstrong, "How I Changed My Mind: Theological Method," *Viewpoint* (September–October 2003), 1, 4.

25 Brian McLaren, *A Generous Orthodoxy* (Grand Rapids, Mich.: Zondervan, 2004), 23.

SCRIPTURE INDEX

ABOUT THE AUTHOR

Dr. John MacArthur is the pastor-teacher of Grace Community Church in Sun Valley, Calif., as well as an author, conference speaker, president of The Master's University and Seminary, and president and featured teacher with the Grace to You media ministry.

In 1969, after graduating from Talbot Theological Seminary, Dr. MacArthur came to Grace Community Church. The emphasis of his pulpit ministry is the careful study and verse-by-verse exposition of the Bible, with special attention devoted to the historical and grammatical background behind each passage. In 1985, Dr. MacArthur became president of The Master's University (formerly Los Angeles Baptist College), an accredited, four-year liberal arts Christian college in Santa Clarita, Calif. In 1986, he founded The Master's Seminary, a graduate school dedicated to training men for full-time pastoral roles and missionary work.

Founded in 1969, Grace to You is the nonprofit organization responsible for developing, producing, and distributing Dr. MacArthur's books, audio resources, and the *Grace to You* radio and television programs. *Grace to You* radio airs more than a thousand times daily throughout the English-speaking world, reaching major population centers with biblical truth.

It also airs nearly a thousand times daily in Spanish, reaching twenty-three countries across Europe and Latin America.

Since completing his first best-selling book *The Gospel according to Jesus* in 1988, Dr. MacArthur has written nearly four hundred books and study guides, including *Our Sufficiency in Christ, Strange Fire, Ashamed of the Gospel, The Murder of Jesus, A Tale of Two Sons, Twelve Ordinary Men, The Truth War, The Jesus You Can't Ignore, Slave, One Perfect Life,* and the MacArthur New Testament Commentary series. His titles have been translated into more than two dozen languages. *The MacArthur Study Bible*, the cornerstone resource of his ministry, is available in English (NKJV, NASB, and ESV), Spanish, Russian, German, French, Portuguese, Italian, Arabic, and Chinese. In 2015, the MacArthur New Testament Commentary series was completed.

John and his wife, Patricia, live in Southern California and have four married children: Matt, Marcy, Mark, and Melinda. They also enjoy the enthusiastic company of their fifteen grandchildren.